br
ok
en

Library of Congress Cataloging-in-Publication Data

Names: Waller, Ryan Casey, author.

Title: Broken / Ryan Casey Waller.

Description: 1 [edition]. | Cincinnati : Forward Movement, 2017. |

Identifiers: LCCN 2017022677 (print) | LCCN 2017024159 (ebook) | ISBN 9780880284417 () | ISBN

Subjects: LCSH: Christian life--Episcopal authors. | Consolation. | Suffering--Religious aspects--Christianity.

Classification: LCC BV4509.5 (ebook) | LCC BV4509.5 .W347 2017 (print) | DDC 248.8/6--dc23

LC record available at https://lccn.loc.gov/2017022677

ISBN: 9780880284417

Printed in USA

Forward
Movement

br ok en

Ryan Casey Waller

Forward Movement
Cincinnati, Ohio

praise
for
broken

Whatever our brokenness may be, the God who has begun a good work in us will not abandon us. In these pages, with honesty, humor, and insight, Ryan Waller testifies faithfully to the movement of God in his life—and in all our lives, if we will only pay attention. *Broken* is a gift to a suffering world.

—**Greg Garrett**
Author of *Entertaining Judgment*
and *The Prodigal*

Ryan has given us a gift in the stories that fill these pages. Eloquent and accessible, honest and insightful, Ryan gives us permission to tell the truth about our doubts, fears, and struggles. His vulnerability reminds us that Christianity is for those of us who feel lost. And his sense of hope encourages us to acknowledge our brokenness, because there we find grace.

—**Julie Rodgers**
Popular blogger and speaker

I have never read a more clear, concise, riveting, hilarious, heart-breaking and life-changing book about a believer dealing with suffering. Ryan doesn't sugarcoat frustrations about God. Instead he opens our eyes to how our love, generosity, and kindness to other people opens our eyes to God's awesome love for us.

Harry H. Harrison Jr.
Best-selling author of *Fearless Parenting* and
Father to Son: Life Lessons on Raising a Boy

table of contents

for Caroline, the one I love

introduction

While they were eating, he took a loaf of bread, and after blessing it he broke it, gave it to them, and said, "Take; this is my body." Then he took a cup, and after giving thanks he gave it to them, and all of them drank from it.

Mark 14:22-23

There is a crack in everything, that's how the lights get in.

Leonard Cohen

Are you ready for your blessing? Are you ready for your miracle?

Chance the Rapper

Dear God, I pray. I had no idea how much pain your children are feeling.

This is my singular thought as I sit reeling from my first few weeks in ministry. *What have I done? I can't handle hearing about all this suffering, much less be expected to do something about it.*

Deep breath.

I can always go back to being a lawyer.

Yes. I repeat these words to myself.

I can always go back to being a lawyer.

I say them again, and the thought begins to soothe the simmer in my brain. *Yes, I can run from God. God won't stop me. God won't even give chase. God doesn't do that sort of thing because God loves free will. Right?*

The image of Jonah trapped in the belly of a stinking fish comes to mind, but I push it away. *God knows I can't handle this line of work. God will understand there's been a terrible mistake. Besides, I'm not Jonah. No great prophet here. God knows exactly who and what I am.*

Broken.

Yes...I can always go back to being a lawyer.

I take another deep breath and read more prayer cards from parishioners in my church.

> "My son is back in rehab with opioid addiction. This is the fourth time. He is 22."
>
> "Last month I was diagnosed with Stage 4 lung cancer. This is exactly how my father died."
>
> "I've been looking for a job for a full year now. No savings left. TERRIFIED."
>
> "I cannot stop looking at pornography. It's making me hate myself. I can't stop."
>
> "Want to be pregnant. Have wanted it for five years. Please pray."
>
> "My child doesn't have a single friend at school. Please, God, send her a friend. Just one."

"Married nineteen years. Husband told me last week he doesn't love me. Hasn't loved me for a long, long time."

I stop reading. I need another breath.

These prayers come from people in the pews of the church I serve. It happens every week. We stock the pews with the prayer cards and ask the congregation to write down anything they'd like for the clergy to pray for on their behalf. We collect the cards during the offering and pray for them on Tuesday mornings. In these first few weeks of my ministry, I learn something: Praying for each other isn't always easy. Prayer is where people get real. We fake it with each another and pretend everything is *fine,* but we usually don't do that with God. We tell God how it is. That's good. Being honest with God is a sign we believe in the power of prayer. If we didn't, we wouldn't bother pouring our hearts out to God.

The problem is nobody else hears our prayers. And in the age of social media, where our lives are curated to show only our best and most beautiful selves, it is easy to believe we are the only ones who are broken.

But we're not. We are all broken and in need of God's blessing. No one has it all together; no person is perfect. Behind our smiles and affirmations that everything is *fine* are gaping wounds of the soul that desperately need the care of a divine physician.

I am learning that we need to pour out our brokenness, not just to God but to each other, so we can know that we are not alone. Something sacred happens when we make ourselves vulnerable to one another—we connect. And in connection, we find healing and life.

John's Gospel offers a provocative moment when Jesus tells his followers they must eat his flesh and drink his blood if they want to have eternal life. John tells us that many people viewed this as a hard teaching and because of it, abandoned Jesus.

Jesus turns to Peter and says, "*Will you leave, too?*

Peter answers, "*Where would I go? You have the words of life.*"

Peter has connected with Jesus and understands that the life he found in Jesus couldn't be found anywhere else. Peter is broken, just like us, but in Jesus he knows he can become something else: blessed.

It has taken me a while to learn this truth: Jesus is the physician my soul needs. So much of religion makes it sound like we need to fix our brokenness before we come to Jesus. But Jesus says just the opposite.

Do you remember what happened on the night Jesus was betrayed?

> While they were eating, he took a loaf of bread, and after blessing it he broke it, gave it to them, and said, "Take; this is my body." Then he took a cup, and after giving thanks he gave it to them, and all of them drank from it.
>
> **Mark 14:22-23**

Did you notice what Jesus did *before* he broke the bread?

He blessed it.

We are all broken in some real way. No person has arrived. No person is whole. We long to be whole, but we are broken, wounded, hurting people. But here is the amazing news of Jesus Christ: he blessed the bread before he broke it. And through Jesus, our brokenness is also blessed, our wounds healed, our hearts made whole.

We may be broken but a current of blessedness runs in the river of our spirit, deeper than our brokenness.

May the words humbly offered in this book give you permission to share your brokenness with others so that you may know you are not alone. May you also remember that you are much more than the sum of your broken parts.

You are something else completely.

A child of God.

And we all know what God does with his children.

God blesses them.

Ryan Casey Waller
Dallas, Texas

help

Be pleased, O God, to deliver me;
O LORD, make haste to help me.

Psalm 70:1

The only thing my mother ever wanted was a family of her own. Her biological father was an alcoholic, and her mother wasn't quite up for the task of raising her as a single mom. So for the first twelve years of her life, my mother was passed between relatives. When her aunt Rachel finally adopted her, Mom said it was the first time in her life she really believed someone loved her.

She married my father shortly before her twentieth birthday with clearly defined goals in mind: to create the family she never had and to shower them with love. And that's exactly what she did. Today, my parents have been married forty-four years. They have four children of their own and ten grandchildren with one more on the way. And while my mother is honest enough to admit there were days she would have happily signed divorce papers, she never did. She stuck it out. She worked it out. She loved and she loved and she loved. My parents both say they are more in love with each other today than they were as teenagers.

Their story, however, is not without its shadows. All families have secrets. Ours is no exception. The trouble is that our secrets tore our family apart.

I know a lot of people who grew up in harsh environments. Like my mother, they were affected by alcoholism or abuse or neglect. If by some chance they were spared these serious maladies, they still experienced all sorts of situations they would rather forget.

I am not one of those people. My childhood was nothing short of idyllic. If you asked me about the worst thing that happened during my childhood, I would have no answer for you. I was spared from suffering. I was surrounded by love. The members of my family were my favorite people on earth. I always had lots of friends, but my best friends were my family. We were as tight and happy a unit as there ever was.

That same family hasn't been under the same roof in years. Not at Thanksgiving. Not at a birthday. Not even for Christmas. The family that my mother dedicated her life to creating and nurturing is utterly broken.

For the sake of those involved, people I dearly love, I will spare you the exact details of the secrets that caused this destruction. For our purposes, it's enough to know the secrets involved money and betrayal. Ultimately, the details of what happened don't really matter. What's done is done. The past cannot be changed. What matters is that some people who once loved each other now hate each other. And that matters a lot, because, unlike the past, this can be changed. Just not by the person we might think.

When my family first broke apart, I was consumed by the desire to fix it. I thought about it constantly, prayed relentlessly, and did everything in my power to "make it all better." I made phone calls, sent texts, begged for us to come together and talk it through. I asked my priest for advice; I asked my therapist for advice; I asked any friend who would listen to tell me what to do. Somebody had to have the answer. It was out there, and I was going to find it.

I carried on like this until one night I woke up with shakes that wouldn't stop. I had become so obsessed with trying to fix my family that I had neglected my own mental, emotional, and spiritual health. It was the first time in my life that I had encountered a problem I couldn't solve. My family was broken, and apparently I was too.

This led me to a dramatic truth about my own faith in God. Up until that point in my life, I had publicly professed God as my Great Helper, all the while quietly believing I could help myself. I proclaimed publicly that I was a helpless sinner who needed the grace of the Lord for salvation. But what I really believed, deep down, was that I could save myself.

Recently I had the opportunity to talk with some people about the pain of addiction. One was a mother who used to pick up her children from school while black-out drunk. Another was a successful businessman who drank in absolute secret. Nobody cared so long as he was winning in the markets. The other was a rich kid who had been given every opportunity in the world only to find himself consumed with hunting down his next pill. They were a diverse group, but they all had one thing in common. They understood the power of asking for help. In the depths of their despair, they asked for help. And, they said, this decision saved them.

What I learned that day is that when a person hits rock bottom, there are only two choices: Stay there. Or get up.

What recovering addicts understand (and what I didn't) is that nobody gets up on her own. Nobody is restored on his own. Nobody is saved on her own.

We all need help.

Whoever wrote Psalm 70 understood this too. *O Lord, make haste to help me.*

I've heard people say that the most authentic prayer is the one that asks for help. So I ask you: When was the last time you asked for help? When was the last time you admitted you couldn't do it alone? When was the last time you fell to your knees and begged God to make haste to help *you*?

I know this is not easy. It's frightening to admit we can't fix it on our own. It feels better to try and believe we have the power to "make it better" because that means all we have to do is work harder and it will happen.

But the truth is that elbow grease and hard work can't always fix a problem. I can't fix my family. Trust me, I tried. It didn't work. *I cannot fix my family.* I have to tell myself this at least once a day. Otherwise, I forget, and I jump right back into the broken cycle of trying.

The good news is that I can ask for help from the One who can fix my family. And even though God has yet to do it—my family is still broken—the simple act of asking has brought me a significant amount of peace. When I declare I can't do it on my own, this acknowledgment allows me to truly trust in the God who can—not just with my lips but with my soul, with every fiber of my being.

A few years ago I delivered a sermon in our church where I told the congregation about a spiritual discipline I learned from author Anne Lamott. She calls the practice "the God Box." Here's how it works. You take out a sheet of paper and you write down a prayer. You ask God for something you really need. Then you put the paper in the box, close the lid, and leave it alone. Once the prayer is inside the box, you are not allowed to touch the box again. The idea is that by physically seeing your hand write down the need, burying it in a box, and letting it go, you will better understand that prayer is about truly giving our concerns to God—and trusting that God will do something about them. God doesn't forget.

I followed Lamott's advice and before I preached the sermon, I put my prayer in a God Box. Then I told the congregation about the experience. What I didn't tell them is what the prayer said. But I'll tell you. This is what I wrote: *God, please heal my broken family of origin.*

A few months after I delivered the sermon, I was moving my God Box from my office to another room when I accidentally dropped it. The lid popped off, and the paper came floating out like a feather, drifting gently to the floor. I picked it up and stared at my messy handwriting for a minute or two.

And then I cried—but not because God has yet to answer the prayer—but because I felt a peace about the situation that I couldn't explain. There I was, reading a prayer that hasn't been answered but feeling completely different about it. We were still broken, but I was a little less broken about it.

I want more than almost anything in the world to see healing within the family my mother and father worked so hard to make. But this may never happen. I cannot control that outcome. It is not for me to control. What I can control—what I'm supposed to control—is who I believe can help solve the problem, who can make whole the broken. Is it me? Or is it God?

My family may never be healed. But my prayer has been heard.

And so I trust, as the psalmist did, that God will not forget to do what God knows I cannot do for myself.

Help.

it's the bible. so what?

It is the spirit that gives life; the flesh is useless. The words that I have spoken to you are spirit and life.

John 6:63

A buddy and I were in a pool hall a few years back, drinking too many cans of lemonade—you know, like friends sometimes do in pool halls on a Friday night. And we got to talking about life, because drinking too many cans of lemonade can make us do such things.

I told him I was thinking about taking seminary classes. We were in law school at the time. He responded like most people did when I told them I was interested in ministry. He tried to talk me out of it.

"Ryan," he said, "let me tell you something. Life's about getting a good job, living in a house you like with people you like. You wake up, go to work, come home, walk the dog, and try to be happy. That's what it comes down to."

"Yeah, that's all fine," I said, "but I feel God's calling me to do this."

"What, exactly? Sit around and talk about the Bible?"

"Maybe. Yeah. I don't really know."

"Do yourself a favor, pal." He took a slug of lemonade. "Don't take the Bible too seriously. Life's complicated enough without trying to figure out the Bible."

Life is complicated, isn't it? Sometimes the temptation in our busy and complicated lives is to be dismissive of the Bible. *I have an electric bill to pay and a promotion to secure. A house to buy and a dog to walk. I'm overcommitted already. I don't exactly have a lot of time for the Bible. Sure, the Bible definitely has some wisdom in it. I get that. But so what? I have stuff to do.*

That's basically what my buddy was asking. *So what?* Why would you read and study the Bible when there are so many other things to do? It's actually not a bad question. In fact, I've dedicated my life to trying to figure out the answer, both for myself and in helping others. Despite my friend's advice, I answered God's call and went to seminary. This year, I was ordained a priest in the Episcopal Church.

As we try to get to the bottom of this question, let's start by saying a few things that the Bible isn't. I like to start from this perspective because I find that a lot of people don't actually know much about the Bible or how it's supposed to be used. After that, I'll say two things about what it is. This won't be comprehensive by any stretch of the imagination, but I think it will be helpful.

First: The Bible isn't a book.

The Bible is a bunch of books. Sixty-six books, to be exact. That's why people like Peter Gomes[1] (a man who was a brilliant biblical scholar) have said the Bible is better described as a library instead of a book.

So when you read a passage from the Bible, some of the first questions to ask are, "What's the genre? Is this poetry? A sermon? History? Doctrine? What is it?" The Bible has all of these (and more), but we can feel overwhelmed if we don't know some context about the words we're reading.

The good news is that you don't have to go to seminary to do this. Good study Bibles have introductions, sidebars, and footnotes that offer plenty of information.[2] Make sure you read these in addition to the scripture. They will give you contexts and perspectives that will enhance your reading. Think of this like doing research before going on vacation. You will have way more fun if you do a little homework before boarding the plane.

But maybe you don't want to read notes in a study Bible. Maybe you hate to read—though that would be a little weird since you're reading this book right now. But if you don't want to read a study Bible or other scholarship to learn about the Bible, then ask someone. Anyone. Seriously, just ask. Everyone is convinced that everyone else knows more about the Bible than they do. They don't.

---

1 Peter Gomes was the longtime chaplain at Harvard University, a genius theologian and preacher. He was an African-American, gay, ordained Baptist minister who voted for Republicans. I tell you this so the next time you think you have someone figured out based upon one label society puts on them, you'll think twice. RIP Pastor Gomes. May light perpetual shine upon you, sir.

2 *The Path* is a good option for this exploration. Condensed and exerpted from the New Revised Standard Version, it features the major stories of the Bible from Genesis to Revelation. Available through Forward Movement.

Don't be embarrassed to ask. Nobody knows it all, but if you ask, you might know a little more afterward. The Bible isn't a book; it's a library. Treat it like that, and you'll have a very rich experience.

Second: The Bible isn't simple.

The Bible is not black and white. And that's perfectly okay. It's not a flight manual.

A woman said to me recently, "I hear you're a preacher."

"Trying to be," I said.

"Let me give you some advice." She smiled in a way that I can only describe as nauseatingly condescending. "Preachers get in trouble when they think too much. God's word is clear and simple. Read it, preach it, and don't get fancy."

I stood there, mentally responding. *I don't think we're reading the same Bible.*

But I'm a wimp, so I just said out loud, "Yes, ma'am."

The Bible is a lot of things, but simple ain't[2] one of them. Take the issue of violence, for example. The Old Testament says: "Thou shall not kill." But then God also commands the Israelites into war and even dictates exactly whom to kill. Flip over to the New Testament where Jesus says: "Turn the other cheek." This leads some Christians to believe that violence is totally off-limits. Others believe that's an absurd position. What about self-defense or the defense of an innocent child or even the notion of a just war?

Same Bible. Different beliefs. This doesn't make truth relative or God fickle. What it means, I think, is that we're not patient enough

---

2 Sorry. I'm from Texas.

to trust that coming to a true understanding takes a lot of time. These issues must be thought through, read in community, and blanketed in prayer. The Bible isn't Google. We don't type in a question and find the answer. It's hard. That's why we read the Bible together within the tradition of the church and pray about what it means. The Bible speaks complex truths about a complex God who loves complex people in a complicated world. If the Bible painted some easy picture of life, I probably wouldn't read it. The Bible rings true because it reflects what *I know* to be true. Life is hard. Life is painful. Life is messy. But in the midst of life, God is present. The Bible is not simple. It contains too much hard truth to be simple.

But even though it's hard, some messages of the Bible are crystal clear. God loves us. God wants to save us. We need to be saved.

Third: The Bible isn't God.

God is way bigger than the Bible—way, way bigger. The Bible, for all its wisdom and beauty and truth, is not to be worshiped. It points to *whom* we worship and guides *how* we worship.

For Episcopalians, this is particularly true. *The Book of Common Prayer*, which guides our worship and practice, is mostly scripture rearranged into different liturgies and prayers. That means everything that happens in our churches is deeply biblical.

With religion, there's always the danger we'll begin to worship our worship. We must remember that God is bigger—bigger than our denomination, bigger than our theology, bigger than our Bible. We have to approach the Bible with humility, never forgetting that God works in ways beyond all we can do or know. We can rightly cherish the Bible and love our worship, but we must remain humble about it. A woman in my church told me recently she was so glad I had left the Baptist church to become a part of the real church, which implied something quite negative about my prior church. I don't think that's the right attitude. Cherish the Bible, love worship, but don't forget that God is very big. And Christians worship God in many good and righteous ways.

So, we're agreed: The Bible isn't a book, it is not simple, and it's definitely not God. *So what the heck is it?*

The Bible is the Word of God.

The Book of Common Prayer has a question and answer section in the back of the book called the Catechism. If you've never looked at it, you should; it starts on page 845. Here's one of the questions: "Why do we call the Holy Scriptures the Word of God?" Answer: "Because God inspired the human authors and because God still speaks to us through the Bible."

Christians argue a lot about the inspiration for the Bible. This is what I think: *The Bible we have is the Bible God wanted us to have.* This is important. The Bible will frustrate and confuse you, and if you don't believe it's the Word God wanted to tell us, you'll be tempted at some point to tune it out. But if it's the Word of God, then each time we read it, we have the chance to hear from the God of the universe. That's tough to ignore.

Ok, one last thought on the Bible. Ready?

The Bible will see you through.

In the lesson from John at the beginning of this essay, the Pharisees ask Jesus about the law. They want to know out of all the commandments which one is the greatest.

Jesus says, "Love the Lord your God with all your heart, and with all your soul, and with all your mind. And love your neighbor as yourself. On these two commandments hang all the law and the prophets."

We often hear that Jesus taught with authority, as someone who really knows what is right. So they say, *Tell us, Jesus, what do we really need to know?* What does he say? This is really important, so don't rush by it. *What's the one thing we really need to know?* How does Jesus answer?

He quotes scripture. He doesn't create a new law. He doesn't tell a parable. He simply stands upon the foundation of his life—the Bible. Take a moment to soak this up.

And this isn't the only time he does this. When Jesus is tempted in the desert, every time Satan comes at him, Jesus responds with scripture. He draws upon its strength and power. He has read the Bible and studied it—and it sustains him in his moments of temptation.

At the end of Jesus' life, as he hangs on a cross, the words of Psalm 22 are on his tongue. "My God, my God, why have you forsaken me?" In his darkest hour, his toughest moments, Jesus relies upon scripture, and like medicine for his soul, it heals him and sees him through to the end.

If it worked for Jesus, it will work for you. And for me.

As I shared earlier, I have been through some rough times with my family. It's been absolutely heartbreaking to see my mother experience the pain of not being able to have her children and grandchildren under the same roof, not even for one night.

During this time, I've begun to wonder whether God really does raise people from the dead. Not in the afterlife, I mean like right now. Does God make all things new? Can God actually do that? In my darker hours, I've been tempted to say *no—it feels too hopeless*. But in the darkness has come something else, ancient words of life—words I've been reading since I was a boy. Words from the psalms like, "What is my hope? O Lord, my hope is in you." Words like, "Though I walk through the valley of the shadow of death, I will fear no evil, for you are with me."

I hear Jesus whispering, "Come to me, all who are weary and heavy-laden and I will give you rest." Then his voice grows louder, more commanding and he says, "I am the resurrection, and the life: he that believeth in me, though he were dead, yet shall he live."

I hear these words of life, turn them over in my soul, and know that I still believe God raises the dead to life. I choose to stand upon the word of God and trust in the promises of the Lord. I believe that when God says he's making all things new, he really is. And when God says there is no person, no relationship, no wreckage he cannot lift from the ruins, I say, "Amen!"

And that's what it comes down to for me. The Bible…so what? *These are words of life, that's what.* And in a world filled with death, this is very, very good news.

finishing what he starts

You then, my child, be strong in the grace that is in Christ Jesus; and what you have heard from me through many witnesses entrust to faithful people who will be able to teach others as well. Share in suffering like a good soldier of Christ Jesus. No one serving in the army gets entangled in everyday affairs; the soldier's aim is to please the enlisting officer. And in the case of an athlete, no one is crowned without competing according to the rules. It is the farmer who does the work who ought to have the first share of the crops. Think over what I say, for the Lord will give you understanding in all things.

2 Timothy 2:1-7

When I was thirteen, I reported to the weight room for my very first workout. Sixth grade was over, and I had the summer to prepare for junior high football. The first order of business was to find out the maximum amount of weight I could lift so the coaches could develop a weight-training program for me.

I should have known this would not go well. A week earlier at the mandatory physical exam, a nurse took my vitals. She noted my height and weight on her notepad.

"Five foot nine…" she said slowly. "One hundred and twenty pounds." She looked up. "The perfect height and weight for a female supermodel."

I don't think that's how Joe Montana's career started.

In the weight room, the coach tells me to lie down on the bench and warm up by pumping the bar a few times. "Don't put any weight on it," he says. "Just the bar. Something easy to get you loose."

"Right," I say. "No problem."

I lie down, grip the bar, and lift it off the rack. I know immediately that I'm in trouble. It takes everything I've got to lower it down to my chest without allowing it to crush me to death.

I heave. Nothing happens. The bar literally doesn't move an inch. But since I can't breathe, I try again. And again nothing happens. By the time the coach rescues me, all eyes are on the kid who can't lift forty-five pounds.

I wanted so badly to be strong. But I wasn't.

In our lesson for this essay, Saint Paul urges Timothy, a young Christian leader, to find strength. We don't know the details but scholars believe Timothy receives this letter in the midst of some kind of personal crisis. In the first chapter of the letter Paul encourages Timothy to not be ashamed of the gospel but to remember that the God who saved him will also see him through.

We must never forget this point. Yes, God has rescued us from sin and death, but God is not through with us. Saved by grace is never the end of a conversation; it is the beginning.

In another letter, this time to the Philippians, Paul says it this way: "I am confident of this, that the One who began a good work among you will bring it to completion" (1:6). You are a work in progress. So am I. Just ask my wife.

Have you ever looked in the mirror and thought, *I'm not the person I imagined I would be?* I have. And it doesn't feel great. If you feel this way, listen to me. This thing isn't over. God is not done with you. There are many days ahead. Days of purpose. Days of hope. Days to become what God has called you to be.

The Bible says, "What we will be has not yet been made known. But we know that when Christ appears, we'll be like Him" (1 John 3:2).

One time, a guy I met at a party asked me if I thought the end of the world was upon us. He was a doomsday kind of guy who seemed a little too eager for the world to end, like he was looking forward to nuclear winter and zombies. "It's only a matter of time," he said, "until the world blows itself up. Watch the news! People just keep getting worse. There's no saving us. It's all gonna blow. But you know what? Then Jesus will come back, so it's cool."

I said, "I'm not really sure about that."

"You don't believe Jesus is coming back?"

"No," I said. "I do. I say it every Sunday in church. Christ has died. Christ is risen. Christ will come again. I believe it. Just not like you do."

"Well, what do you believe?"

I thought for a moment. Then I said, "I believe God finishes what he starts. When God created us, he said we were good. And when we got off track, God came to fix us, to redeem us. Yes, Christ will someday return in glory but Christ's kingdom has also *already* come, and with it the opportunity for us to partner with Christ and experience redemption here and now by acting as instruments of peace and love in this world. Redemption is what I hope for. Redemption is what I believe in."

Theologian N.T. Wright describes this tension that Christians live in as the "already and the not yet." Jesus made God's kingdom present on earth, but because we continue to groan under the weight of sin and death, we don't fully experience redemption—being saved from our sinfulness—in this life. But someday, somehow, we will.

God has a plan for your life. God will finish the good work God has begun in you. But it takes time. Faith isn't a steady climb toward perfection—there are valleys and deserts along the way. If you stick with faith long enough, you're guaranteed to experience hardships just like Timothy.

There will be dog days. There's no other way to say it. Life will get rough. Some people will experience doubt. Believing will suddenly become hard. For others, it will become boredom. As a teenager, I was afraid that if I followed Jesus, my life would be boring. Life would become some never-ending Sunday school class where I had to be an eternally good boy. And I didn't want to be that. Honestly, I still don't want to be that. I'm *not* that.

For others like my doomsday friend, the world seems too dark for faith. And I get that. On the afternoon of September 11, I turned on my car and heard Coldplay singing these lyrics: *We live in a beautiful world…We live in a beautiful world…*

I punched the radio off and said a few words you probably don't want me to repeat. I didn't want to hear that song because nothing seemed beautiful that day. Sometimes the world is so bleak that we just don't want to hear about God stuff.

Crisis is part of life, which means it's part of faith. Deserts and valleys are normal. They're okay. The mistake—and it's a dangerous one—is confusing a crisis of faith with the end of faith.

The first thing Paul does in our lesson from Timothy is point to the source of his strength: grace in Christ. God's grace allows us to have faith. It is a gift, something we cannot create. Yet, after faith's creation, we can strengthen it through effort and practice. A teacher of mine liked to say that grace is opposed to earning, but not to effort. Earning is for Jesus. Effort is for us. In other words, God gives grace, and then it's up to us to nurture it.

Paul offers three images to help us understand this concept: A soldier devoted to his cause, an athlete devoted to her rules, and a farmer devoted to his work.

All three evoke effort. A soldier has duty; an athlete, discipline; and the farmer has work ethic. This is Paul's version of a Nike commercial. *Just do it!* Having a faith crisis? Doubting? Bored? Discouraged? Pray harder! Fast longer! Sing louder! *Just do it! Just have more faith!*

This kind of talk is helpful. Sometimes. All of us from time to time need a good kick in the pants. But other times, I just can't hear this stuff. I don't want to hear it, because frankly, I want God to *just do it* for me, just step in and solve my problems.

A mentor of mine named Father Greg says one of the more dangerous sins we commit is spiritual greed. He defines spiritual greed as expecting mind-blowing miracles every second of the day. It's not that they don't happen; they do. But most days are a slow progression forward, not a rocket blast to the moon. Put another way: Most days are workdays, not reward days. That is probably good. Isn't it through the work that we prepare for the reward?

Muhammad Ali, the late, great boxer, said he ran the long road before he ever danced under the lights. Famous scientist Albert Einstein said it wasn't that he was all that much smarter than anybody else—he was just willing to sit with problems longer.

I know a guy who spent the last few years trying to make the Olympic bobsled team. This dude is a tremendous athlete. He played in the National Football League before he became interested in bobsledding. He spent months training in Canada, hundreds of miles from his wife and young child.

Before the last Winter Olympics, he missed making the Olympic team by seconds. Can you imagine? I asked him about it. I expected anger, maybe even some tears. But all he wanted to talk about was the training he was doing for the next race.

Mind. Blown.

There's something to be admired about that kind of endurance. I think it's what Paul is getting at when he instructs us to endure hardship like an athlete, a soldier, and a farmer. These are people willing to work hard and wait patiently for the results.

Faith is bizarre. So often when we hit a valley or a desert, our reaction is to back off. Our prayer life begins to feel hollow, so we stop praying. Church feels rigid, so we leave and take up Sunday brunch instead. Faith becomes distasteful, so we feed on something else. We don't do that with our jobs or our relationships. We don't even do it with our hobbies. When we discover weakness, we increase our effort. We give the things we struggle with more attention, not less.

Mother Teresa confessed that she went years without feeling the presence of God. All the while, she toiled away helping the poorest of the poor in the slums of Calcutta. How could she carry on with her ministry for so many years without feeling the presence of God? What gave her strength? Maybe Mother Teresa simply believed Paul when he said the One who began a good work in her would finish it.

Our question becomes: *Do you believe that? Are you willing to work and wait, trusting that God keeps his promises? That God finishes what he starts? Are you willing to endure everything, as Paul does, for the sake of Christ?*

I honestly don't know if I am. On my good days, I think, *Maybe.*

But here's the thing. The athlete, soldier, and farmer have something else besides their strength in common. Each one toils with a vision in mind.

> For the soldier: a victory.

> For the athlete: a gold medal.

> For the farmer: a harvest.

Saint Paul says to be strong but to remember Jesus Christ. Remember the One who remains faithful even when we aren't. Remember the One who won't deny us because he can't deny himself. Remember the source of our strength: grace in Jesus Christ.

There are times to pull on our boots and lean harder into faith. There are also times when our tank is empty. Sometimes the valley is too deep and the desert too dry, and we just can't pull off a glib Nike commercial.

Sometimes our crisis doesn't stem from boredom or a theological conundrum but the death of our mother, the end of our marriage, or, God forbid, cancer in our precious child. In these moments all we can manage are the few steps needed to stumble into the open arms of Jesus.

And you know what?

That's okay. It's fine.

Jesus doesn't measure our faith before accepting us. He simply says to come. *Come back to me*, he pleads. *Come back to me. I'll carry you the rest of the way. I'll give you the strength you need.*

After that first day in the gym, I never wanted to go back. But I did. Because I couldn't lift the bar, the coach instructed me to use one of the weight plates for my exercises. It weighed thirty-five pounds. It was embarrassing.

An older, popular boy named Jack walked in and saw what I was doing. "No, Ryan, you're supposed to put that thing on the bar. Here, let me show you."

I sat up fast. "I know, but coach told me to do it like this."

"Why?"

"Because…" I whispered. "I can't lift the bar. This is all I can do."

Jack eyed me a long moment. He glanced at the other boys, all of whom were staring. "Oh yeah," Jack said. "Yeah, of course." He slapped me on the back. "Keep it up then. You're doing fine." I went back to lifting. So did everyone else.

Life is heavy, and our faith doesn't always feel strong enough to endure it. *But keep it up. You're doing fine.*

If you keep moving toward God, either at a sprint or in a crawl, I promise you will make it. I promise. You will make it.

How do I know?

Because. God finishes what he starts.

do
what
you can

It was two days before the Passover and the festival of
Unleavened Bread. The chief priests and the scribes were
looking for a way to arrest Jesus by stealth and kill him; for
they said, "Not during the festival, or there may be a riot
among the people."

While he was at Bethany in the house of Simon the leper,
as he sat at the table, a woman came with an alabaster jar
of very costly ointment of nard, and she broke open the jar
and poured the ointment on his head. But some were there
who said to one another in anger, "Why was the ointment
wasted in this way? For this ointment could have been sold
for more than three hundred denarii, and the money given
to the poor." And they scolded her. But Jesus said, "Let her
alone; why do you trouble her? She has performed a good
service for me. For you always have the poor with you, and
you can show kindness to them whenever you wish; but you
will not always have me. She has done what she could; she has
anointed my body beforehand for its burial. Truly I tell you,
wherever the good news is proclaimed in the whole world,
what she has done will be told in remembrance of her."

Mark 14:1-9

In college, a friend and I were standing in line to order
dinner when a deaf woman approached us, hands out,
clearly wanting money. Clumsily, I tried to communicate
that I didn't have cash but was more than happy to buy
her a meal. As I gestured furtively, my friend Jason did
something unexpected.

He began communicating in sign language. Soon, the two were conversing in a language I didn't understand. But I understood what happened next. They finished their conversation, hugged one another, and the woman walked away—her spirits clearly lifted by the experience.

Jason had never said a word to me about knowing sign language. I mean, this was a guy who was more likely to be found surfing than studying. So when the woman left, I said, "What was that?"

"What?"

"The sign language, dude?"

"Oh, that. I noticed that woman hanging around, and she looked lonely. So I thought I'd do something about it."

"So, you learned sign language?"

"Well…I'm trying to," Jason said. "I'm not fluent. I'm just doing what I can."

I was dumbfounded. His actions seemed extreme and completely unexpected. I didn't know what to make of it.

I'm just doing what I can. Who says that? Who does that?

A few weeks later, my landlord Letty stopped by. Jason happened to be at my house at the time. Letty was from South America, and while she spoke English fairly well, she was far more comfortable in Spanish. As we were discussing some repairs that needed to be made, Jason did it again. Without warning, he started speaking Spanish. At this point, I figured he was a spy.

I stepped aside and let the two of them have their moment. Letty's eyes lit up as Jason spoke to her in her native tongue. And as with the conversation with the deaf woman, this one also ended with hugs. Afterward, Jason confessed to me that he had been learning Spanish so he could get to know some of the underprivileged kids in our neighborhood, most of whom spoke only Spanish. I was beyond confused. Why was he going to all this trouble for strangers?

I know what you're thinking. Jason must be some sort of genius who can learn languages in the blink of an eye. (I am currently reading a book written by a woman who speaks nine languages. Nine!) That sort of thing is certainly possible. But here's the thing about Jason—he applied to our college three times before being admitted. He isn't a genius; he's something better. He's generous. Outrageously so.

Our lesson from Mark tells of a woman who reminds me of my friend. The story tells of a woman who does what she can. A woman who gives so generously that it confuses and even angers those around her.

We find Jesus in Bethany, dining at the home of Simon the leper during a most precarious hour of his life. In the preceding passage, the chief priests plot to kill Jesus. And just after this scene, Judas will throw his lot in with these same men and begin searching for an opportunity to betray his teacher.

Jesus has, quite literally, come to the end of his road. Jerusalem and a Roman cross loom only two miles away. There is little time left.

The pressure is mounting, the anxiety thickening. A few verses later Jesus will fall to the ground, grieving to the point of death. The Bible says his tears were like blood. He'll keep himself awake all night, praying desperately to God, begging to not die.

But for now he sits down for a meal, and we imagine he is anything but relaxed. We see deep grooves of stress cutting sharply across his forehead, and worry clouds the whites of his eyes. If we saw Jesus on this night, most of us would turn and pretend we did not see this troubled man. That's what I probably would do. A person in deep distress is an uncomfortable person to be around; it is much easier to ignore the person and carry on with our own business.

And that's when the woman appears, anonymous and silent, bearing a costly, outrageously generous gift.

In her hands is an alabaster jar filled with nard, a soothing perfume and an expensive one too—by some accounts, worth a whole year's wages. In the Song of Songs, nard is described as an ointment that emits a sweet fragrance for the king's banquet. At the end of a life, nard is applied to the corpse in preparation for burial. Nard is expensive, useful, and precious.

The woman enters the room, and without warning, she shatters the jar, pouring the perfume onto the head of Jesus. It flows down his head and hair and onto his face. Its sweetness permeates the whole room.

Close your eyes and imagine this; visualize the intimacy and sacredness of such a scene. Smell the nard.

Jesus sits at the table, exhausted from a three-year tour of non-stop ministry. He has traveled incessantly, been rejected in his hometown, cast out demons, and brought the dead back to life. His body is stiff, his feet are calloused, and his heart is burdened by all he has seen. And now his mind is filled with terror about what lies ahead.

And then this angel of woman appears and blesses his body. She spreads the nard into his hair. Her fingers massage his scalp. Her hands work their way from his head, to his neck, to his shoulders.

She takes her time. She is focused.

Jesus' breathing slows; he begins to relax. He closes his eyes and allows the only woman in the room to grant him respite from his troubles. But even as this woman blesses Jesus, Judas sits at the same table looking for a chance to betray him. Can you feel the tension?

Judas isn't the only one at the table with dark thoughts whirling through his brain. The rest of the men at dinner do not like what they see, either.

Don't waste the ointment! one of the disciples cries out. The Greek literally puts it this way: "Why this destruction?" The murmurs grow louder. *The nard could be sold for a tremendous amount of money—money that could be given to the poor! How dare you?*

The woman says nothing. She focuses only on Jesus. He is the sole reason she is here. For the moment, he is the only person in her world.

Most of the time, Mark's Gospel portrays the disciples as bumbling idiots who can't seem to understand what Jesus is trying to say or do. But in this instance, they have a point, don't they. To pour out this perfume seems wasteful since we're told the perfume has the value of a year's wages. A full year!

The median annual income in the United States is $51,000. Imagine someone walking into a dinner party and uncorking a $51,000 bottle of wine and offering it to only one person to drink? That would raise a few eyebrows, right? You can imagine how people would respond if the lucky guest took a single sip and then poured the rest of it on the floor.

I was once in the home of a fabulously wealthy man who went to great lengths to show me the grandeur of all his possessions. And I have to admit, it was pretty fun. Who doesn't enjoy a mansion, resort-style pool, and a garage filled with exotic automobiles? I would be lying if I said I wasn't at least momentarily seduced by the opulence.

By the end of the tour, however, I found myself troubled. Like the disciples, I couldn't help but wonder how his wealth might have been better used. I mean, how many children could be fed for the price of a Ferrari and a few Mercedes and BMWs? 1,000? 10,000? 100,000? I honestly don't know.

The United Nations reports that one in every eight humans on earth goes to bed hungry. If you're wondering, that's 870 million people a day who don't have enough food to eat.

The disciples must be thinking about the same math in their day. It's nearly Passover, a time when special concern is focused on almsgiving—offering food and money to the poor. The jar of alabaster could have been a tremendous blessing for others. Instead, the woman pours the perfume on the head of Jesus and leaves the dregs dripping onto the floor.

The disciples' outrage has some merit. Why the waste? Like my friend learning foreign languages for the benefit of strangers, this woman strikes me as extreme. Surely this story isn't telling us to waste our resources in such a way? Surely we're not called to imitate the actions of this woman? Are we? We can't easily dismiss the story, though. Jesus declares that whenever the gospel is proclaimed, her story shall be told. And here we are, more than 2,000 years later, proclaiming the gospel—and this story. So what do we make of our generous woman?

"Let her alone," Jesus says. "Why do you trouble her? She has done a beautiful thing for me."

In other words: Stop your pragmatic calculations and appreciate the beauty of what's happening. Beauty. To a practical mind, beauty isn't all that useful. Elizabeth Nordquist, a Presbyterian pastor and spiritual director, says, "For the economist, beauty does not balance the numbers. For the activist, beauty does not advance the cause. For the strategist, beauty does not give the upper hand."

But for Jesus, beauty matters. What is it about this moment that is so beautiful to Jesus?

Jesus says, "You always have the poor with you, and whenever you will, you can do good to them; but you will not always have me."

This is one of the most misunderstood verses in all of the New Testament. He is not saying poverty is inevitable. Let me repeat this: Jesus is *not* saying poverty is inevitable. I think Jesus is saying: *Give me a break! Get your nose out of the air and stop pretending to be so pious. You already have instructions to care for the poor. Follow the the instructions. Help the poor.*

But right now, I'm with you in a way that I soon won't be. And this woman, in acknowledging my presence in her life, has acted boldly and outrageously in faith.

What's beautiful to Jesus is that the woman *sees him*. She notices his pain and does something about it. But the disciples, blinded by their plans and rigidness, miss the point.

I wonder how many times I miss the point of a story or experience. I wonder how many people I miss.

I was jogging down a busy street in Dallas a few years ago when I tripped and fell. It was one of those falls when you immediately know that you are going all the way down. I may or may not have said an unholy word on my descent to the concrete. I still have a scar on the palm of my hand. As I sprawled on the ground, bloodied and embarrassed by the gawking onlookers, a teenager appeared above me. I had seen him across the street moments before I went down.

"Are you all right?" he asked. He offered me his hand and helped me get to my feet. "Do you need help walking home?"

I glanced back at all the people staring at me from their cars and then looked back at the kid. He could have just kept walking. He could have looked the other way and pretended he didn't see me. It would have been so easy. But he didn't do that. Instead, he ran across the street to help.

It seems like a small thing, I know. But it's not. That kid's generosity and his willingness to help touched me in a deep way. He saw me fall and did what he could to help me up.

The visual of our gospel lesson is stunning in its extravagance, but the real beauty resides in our woman's openness to God, in her willingness to help. That's beauty.

We often think of generosity only in terms of our personal capacity to give. *How much can we give?* That isn't a bad question. But it's not *the* question. Our generosity can become trapped in a prison of our own calculations. Perhaps a better starting point is to inquire about our generosity to God. Perhaps the real question is: *How open are we to God?*

The disciples aren't wrong; their instincts are correct. We should govern our finances in such a manner that we maximize our ability to serve others. But when our calculations drown the voice of God in our lives, we have a problem. If there's one thing I know for sure it's that God will surprise us.

Nobody expects a woman to shatter a $50,000 bottle of perfume over the head of Christ. But she does, and he likes it. Likewise, no one expects the Son of God to lay down his life for the world, but he does.

Years ago, my friend Jason and I were driving through Los Angeles when he suddenly pulled the car over to speak with a man begging on a street corner. After a few words, Jason flung open the door and invited the man into the car. I know some people are comfortable with this sort of thing, but I'm not; I was terrified. Jason assured me that he knew this guy, and it turned out he did. For the next hour, we drove this man around town to various shops, allowing him to run his errands much faster than on foot.

Afterward, Jason said, "Look, I don't do that all the time, but I try hard not to forget about him. I can't offer that guy much, but I can help him run his errands."

My friend does what he can. The woman in Mark's lesson does what she can. I worry about me.

What about you? Do you worry about you?

I am comforted to imagine that as Jesus hangs on the cross, suffering, his mind escapes to the memory of this woman's hands on his head. I like to believe her blessing eases his suffering, if only for a few moments.

There are people in need all around us, but do we see them? Will we do what we can? Will we be extravagant in our generosity? Will we embody beauty in our giving?

I don't know. But I can't think of anything I'd rather hear Jesus say about my life than what he says about this woman: *She did what she could. And it was beautiful.*

just
one
night

Jesus, full of the Holy Spirit, returned from the Jordan and was led by the Spirit in the wilderness, where for forty days he was tempted by the devil. He ate nothing at all during those days, and when they were over, he was famished. The devil said to him, "If you are the Son of God, command this stone to become a loaf of bread." Jesus answered him, "It is written, 'One does not live by bread alone.'" Then the devil led him up and showed him in an instant all the kingdoms of the world. And the devil said to him, "To you I will give their glory and all this authority; for it has been given over to me, and I give it to anyone I please. If you, then, will worship me, it will all be yours." Jesus answered him, "It is written, 'Worship the Lord your God, and serve only him.'" Then the devil took him to Jerusalem, and placed him on the pinnacle of the temple, saying to him, "If you are the Son of God, throw yourself down from here, for it is written, 'He will command his angels concerning you, to protect you,' and 'On their hands they will bear you up, so that you will not dash your foot against a stone.'" Jesus answered him, "It is said, 'Do not put the Lord your God to the test.'" When the devil had finished every test, he departed from him until an opportune time.

Luke 4:1-13

When Apple released the second-generation iPhone, my sister asked if I wanted to buy one. And like every other Millennial who's ever been asked that question, I replied, "Is that seriously even a question? Just tell me when and where."

"Good," she said. "You have to come and wait in line with me tomorrow at the store. It's gonna take a while."

"Totally worth it," I said. I was in graduate school at the time, so I didn't have much else to do but study. I figured I would knock out some reading while we waited. When we got to the store, I discovered my sister hadn't been exaggerating. The line wrapped all the way around the building. You've probably seen the pictures: a bunch of hipster-techie-nerds lined up, acting like kids on Christmas. So we stood there and talked and waited.

But after a few hours, a thought began to creep in my head. *This is kind of dumb.* Just then a car pulled up, and the driver hung his head out the window and yelled, "Hey! Morons! You guys know it's just a *phone*, right?" Then he peeled off.

All the people in line were like, "Whatever, dude! It's so much more than a phone. It's an iPhone! And Steve Jobs is a god!"

All I could think was, *That dude is totally right. It is just a phone. And we are a bunch of morons.*

But you know how it is when you want something. You want it! I wanted that phone. I *still* want the latest iPhone.

You know what I'm talking about. You test drive a new Jeep and feel the warm sun on your face. Or you slip a watch on your wrist or those shoes on your feet, and you're a goner. So what if your Corolla is paid off, your Timex keeps perfect time, and your closet is already filled with Nikes. You want things! So you buy them!

Consumerism is a battle we all fight. The enemy in this battle is the voice in our head always telling us we need more. We know the voice is lying, yet it's hard to resist that voice, the one that taunts you, tells you that you need it or deserve it or that this purchase will be the last. *Promise.* And the voice is so ridiculously convincing. I have believed it many times.

Part of what it means to be a Christian is to take seriously the idea that we ought to have less. We are called to live into the paradox that in having less, we'll find more.

So we fast. We tithe. We don't take all we can from the marketplace. We leave things on the table, we give good things away, and we do not measure our lives by how much stuff we can jam into the garage.

In today's lesson, Jesus is about to begin his public ministry. To prepare for the journey ahead, he enters the desert for forty days to pray and fast. While he's doing with less, the devil comes and tempts him, telling Jesus that what he needs is not fasting and prayer, but *more*: more food, more comfort, more power.

Turn these stones to bread, the devil says. *You need to eat.*

Bread doesn't sustain my life, Jesus says. *God does.*

The devil tries again. *Jesus, you know I command the hearts and minds of many people. But, if you were to make me your god, I'd share.*

There is only one God I worship.

The devil makes one last pass at Jesus. *Why are you even doing this? Call the angels to rescue you. You can be comfortable within seconds! You have the power. Why not use it?*

Stop testing God, Jesus replies. *It's a bad idea.* I can totally see Jesus wagging his finger at this point.

And with that, Luke says the devil gives up and leaves Jesus alone to pray and fast.

Remember those bracelets from a few years ago, the ones with W.W.J.D. printed on them? (What Would Jesus Do?) The idea was to wear the bracelet and ask yourself what Jesus would do in every situation. Nice idea, I guess. The problem is that it sets an impossible standard. What would Jesus do? Probably not what I'm about to do!

Seriously. Who can be like Jesus in every moment? Nobody. That's what makes him Jesus and us *us*. The better question to explore is: What would Jesus do to get himself ready? Think of it this way. If a kid sees Michael Phelps winning gold medals in the swimming pool and asks his mom or dad how he can be like Phelps, what do the parents say? *Jump in the pool and swim fast?* No. They say, *Jump in the pool and train for years and years and years.* If a kid wants to be like Michael Phelps, then he has to be willing to prepare like Michael Phelps.

It's the same thing with our faith. We won't have a chance to do what Jesus did unless we prepare like him. We won't have the willpower to say no to more, to quiet that voice of want and desire, unless we have done some strength training. Until we practice again and again and experience what it's like to live—and be satisfied—with less, we will continue to give in to every whim and whimsy. This passage from Luke gives us a training plan by showing us how Jesus practices saying No to *more*.

Jesus is readying himself to embark on the most important work in the history of humanity.

So, first he takes time to prepare his mind, body, and soul with a period of fasting and prayer. As he fasts and prays, he encounters the frailty of his own body and psyche.

His ministry will be difficult, and temptation and struggle will litter his path to Jerusalem and the cross. He will experience moments of weakness, frustration, and even anger, but Jesus decides once and for all that he will look to God and the Holy Scriptures for his sustenance and guidance when trouble comes. But his preparation is tested almost immediately with the temptations offered by the devil.

Will Jesus believe the devil's promise that the answer to his troubles can be found in *more* or will he trust that in God the Father, he already has enough? When confronted with the complexities of life, will Jesus seek more comfort and power? Or, will he know that in resisting *more*, he will see how much he already has?

This is the choice. And it's the same one we have today. To seek more? Or to trust that God has already given us enough?

Jesus chooses the latter. What will we choose?

Jesus fasts and he prays. He cuts out the excess, and he turns down the noise. And at the end of forty days, he emerges from the desert prepared, ready to do what God is calling him to do. Ready because he knows, *really knows*, he has everything he needs for the journey.

Do you know that? Do you know that God promises you a peace that passes all understanding? Do you know that God promises wisdom to handle any complexity? Do you know God promises a love that will never forsake you? Do you *really* know these promises? Or is your life so full of *more* that you can't know these promises?

It's that's the case, it's okay. My life is so full that sometimes all I can do is scrape together a few seconds with Jesus. Then my phone pings, a baby cries, or I realize I forgot to write an email. And off I go. Knowing but *not really* knowing. I end up filling myself with so many things—and the promise of more things—that I don't have any room left for Jesus.

We can't eat nourishing food if we're already filled with junk. And we can't taste sweet wine when we're already drunk.

Consumerism—this false promise of *more*—is an insatiable beast. And you can feed it. Hell, you *will* feed it. We all do. I recently bought a pair of shoes I did not need. I knew it the second I clicked buy. Instant guilt. You know the kind. When the box arrived, my wife just looked at me. She didn't say a word. She didn't have to. I was instantly transported back to that line outside the Apple store. I was reminded that temptation is a lifelong battle. The desire for *more* is a temptation that never goes away. Comedian Jim Carrey says everybody should get rich and famous and do everything they ever dreamed of so they can see that money and fame are not the answers to happiness and fulfillment.

The answers are not found in *more* but in the God who comes to us in the desert—the God who makes sure we don't eat stones but bread, the God who sustains us with what we actually need—love, peace, wisdom, and salvation. God the Father of Abraham, Isaac, Jacob, Sarah, Rebecca, Leah, and Rachel loves his children and forever promises to give us what we need.

But we will never experience the fulfillment of this promise if we are always looking for *more*. We must choose our path—our method for living, for choosing. God? Or *more*?

Years ago my mother met a family who had chosen their method for life. My mom has been a flight attendant for twenty-five years, and like any person in the airline industry, she has some stories. And I mean *stories*. You wouldn't believe what she's seen happen at thirty-thousand-feet.

This particular incident happened years ago, back when a full meal was included in a ticket for coach class.

A family boards the plane for a flight from Dallas to Orlando. Mom. Dad. Four kids—all holding brown paper bags. It turns out this was their first flight. Nobody in the family has ever been on an airplane before. So, naturally, they have brought their lunches. They don't know any better.

When my mom arrives at their row, she explains they can have a hot meal if they want it. No extra charge. The family can't believe it. Mom starts serving them and asks, "What's in Orlando? Y'all going on vacation?"

The faces of the children lit up. "Yes!" they said. "Disney World!"

"Oh, that'll be so fun. How long are you staying?"

The mother and father share a quick look. A slight tension fills the air, and Mom immediately regrets the question.

"One day," the father finally said. "We're flying home tomorrow."

Mom glances at the children. They are listening to the conversation. One day in Disney.

My mom said that not a flicker of light faded from their eyes. They were happy. They were as grateful to be heading to the Magic Kingdom as anyone in the history of that place. Mom said they simply oozed gratitude and contentment.

One night in Disney World? Are you kidding me? I would have told my parents to shove it. I was such a brat. I'm still a brat.

Not those kids. They had a method for life.

I don't know what the method was. I don't know if they believed in God. I don't know anything about them other than they knew what Jesus knows. The answer isn't found in *more*.

I don't know what their answer was to the question of *more*, but I have a suspicion. Saint Augustine said, "Thou hast made us for thyself, and our heart is restless until it finds its rest in thee."

Author C.S. Lewis called it a God-shaped vacuum that only God can fill.

What are you longing for? The next promotion? A bigger house? Fancier car? Can any of those fill the vacuum of your soul?

We only get to be here so long. Time moves very fast. Don't waste it. Don't get to the end of your journey only to discover you never chose a method.

Jesus knew his Father had given him enough.

May you know it too.

you
are
enough

Jesus left that place and went away to the district of Tyre and Sidon. Just then a Canaanite woman from that region came out and started shouting, "Have mercy on me, Lord, Son of David; my daughter is tormented by a demon." But he did not answer her at all. And his disciples came and urged him, saying, "Send her away, for she keeps shouting after us." He answered, "I was sent only to the lost sheep of the house of Israel." But she came and knelt before him, saying, "Lord, help me." He answered, "It is not fair to take the children's food and throw it to the dogs." She said, "Yes, Lord, yet even the dogs eat the crumbs that fall from their masters' table." Then Jesus answered her, "Woman, great is your faith! Let it be done for you as you wish." And her daughter was healed instantly.

Matthew 15:21-28

Have you ever been left out? Told you weren't smart enough for the job? Not pretty enough for the clique? Ever just been flat-out ignored, overlooked, or rejected? Marilyn Monroe said she sometimes felt like her whole life had been one big rejection.

I've felt this way. Have you? Have you felt that no matter what you did it was never going to be good enough? If you have, I want you to read the next line very carefully.

It's not true.

You are enough.

Our God says you're perfectly and wonderfully made. God wants you to know this. But if you don't, do me a favor: Put down this book and go ask somebody. Ask a friend, a therapist, your spouse. Ask your mom, your dad, just ask somebody. *Am I good enough? Am I pretty enough? Am I smart/strong/faithful enough?*

Can you help me to feel better about myself? Can you help me to love myself again, to believe that I am enough?

Asking for help is never weakness. It is always strength.

As a kid, I learned a little about strength by playing baseball. I was never a good athlete, but I loved the game and everything about it—the dirt, the grass, the surge of adrenaline when bat connected with ball. And is there anything in the world that beats the thrill of diving headfirst for home plate? I *loved* the game of baseball.

Some of my best memories are of playing catch with my faither. I replay these scenes when I need to remember something golden. With my father, it never mattered how hard I threw the ball or whether I could even catch the thing (most of the time I couldn't). That never mattered. We just threw the ball back and forth, and it was marvelous.

In ninth grade, my coach sat me down and told me I hadn't made the team. He said I wasn't good enough to play baseball anymore. I went to a small school—only three boys were cut from the team.

I sat on my bedroom floor that night, staring at my brand new cleats. I felt guilty my parents had spent money on shoes I would never use. The shine of the untarnished leather taunted me all night long. The next morning I put them in the back of my closet where they stayed for years. I never threw them out. I don't really know why I kept them. But I did. And it hurt every time I saw them. Sometimes when I came home from college, I would look at the cleats and imagine what it would have been like to play on the team.

It was just a silly baseball team, but it hurt—it always hurts to be left out. We human beings long to be included, don't we? We love to be told *You belong!* The bummer is that most of the time we're told that we *don't.*

> *I'm sorry but you don't qualify for this loan.*
>
> *I hate to break it to you—you're a hard worker—but we have to let you go.*
>
> *I promised to love you forever, but things have changed. I've changed. It's over.*

In life, there are endless moments of rejection—endless moments to believe we are less than we are.

In our lesson for this chapter, a Gentile woman comes to see Jesus. She believes, and perhaps has been told by others, that she is worth very little. Matthew says the woman brings her sick daughter to Jesus, saying, "Have mercy on me, Lord, Son of David."

And Jesus ignores her. "He did not answer her at all," is what the Bible actually says. Take careful note of this. It's very unusual for Jesus to simply ignore people.

My wife and I went out for frozen yogurt a few years back, and we saw Hall of Fame quarterback Troy Aikman grabbing takeout from the restaurant next door. We brushed shoulders on the sidewalk, and I whispered in his ear, "You're the greatest."

Troy turned and laughed. I nearly fell over because I couldn't believe my childhood hero had given me even one second of his time.

One second is all this woman wants from Jesus. A second of attention, a drop of mercy. She's not looking for an autograph or a laugh; she's looking for *life*.

But the disciples aren't having it. She's a Gentile, and they're Jews, and she's annoying them. *Send her away,* they say. *Shut her up!*

This is not a pretty scene. But it's going to be okay because Jesus is here. *I know he is ignoring her, but he'll do the right thing. This is Jesus we're talking about.*

Jesus replies, "I was sent only to the lost sheep of the house of Israel."

Seriously, Jesus? Maybe I misheard you. Did you just give this woman the cold shoulder?

Sorry, Jesus says, *I'd love to help, but I've only got so much time and so much power. I've come for my people first. Yours will have to wait.*

The woman falls to her knees. "Lord, help me," she pleads.

All right. Come on, Jesus! Look, I know you're tired. Maybe you're having a bad day? It happens to all of us. But she's on her knees. And you're Jesus. Do the right thing. Please.

Nope, he says. "It is not fair to take the children's food and throw it to the dogs."

All right. Now we've gone too far. Did you just call her a dog? I'm pretty sure you just called her a dog.

What is going on here? Jesus, why would you say something so disgustingly offensive?

Okay. Take a deep breath. I know I need one. Every single time I read this story, I get fired up. But a little bit of context helps simmer me down. At this point in Matthew, Jesus is in Tyre and Sidon. These are Gentile cities whose inhabitants are described as the Jews' bitter enemies. Many Jewish peasants living in Galilee have been forced to grow food for the rich Gentiles living in Tyre and Sidon. So when this woman comes asking for a healing, it's doubly offensive to the disciples because she belongs to the class of people who are oppressing them. How dare she ask Jesus for a miracle?

We also know Jesus has just fed the five thousand, walked on water, and endured yet another heated argument with the Pharisees. The man must be exhausted. He's probably come to Tyre and Sidon to catch his breath. And then up walks this woman—one more person asking something of him.

Jesus says, *Look, maybe you can be fed too but not before the children. Children eat before dogs.*

I don't know about you, but even with context this is a tough thing for me to hear Jesus say. But we need to hear it because this is where the story gets good.

Groveling on her knees, the Gentile woman says, "Yes, Lord, yet even the dogs eat the crumbs that fall from their masters' table."

You're right, she says. *I'm just a dog, a nobody. I don't belong at your table. I just want to lick your floor. I just want to eat your crumbs.*

"Woman," Jesus says, "great is your faith! Let it be done for you as you wish." And it is done. Her daughter is healed.

This is the only passage in the Bible where someone appears to get the best of Jesus in a theological argument. The scribes can't touch him. His disciples never have a chance. But this woman, a Gentile dog like you and me speaks truth to power.

And maybe this is what Jesus has wanted all along. Maybe he hasn't come to Tyre and Sidon for a rest. Maybe he is here for something much, much bigger. Think about it. If Jesus simply heals the woman's daughter, what will the disciples learn? Most likely, they will just be offended and then forget about the whole incident.

But hearing *her*—this interloper—give the right answer? Hearing *her* speak truth about grace? Now we're going someplace interesting, learning something about this God who so loves the world that he sends his only begotten Son to save it.

Through this encounter, Jesus forces the disciples to view Gentiles in a breathtaking new way. Never again can they assume who God will save and who God won't. Never again can they draw a line in the sand based on gender, skin color, or ethnicity. The disciples believe this woman is incapable of having great faith. But Jesus says she does.

She isn't one of them. It turns out she is something better. She is one of God's.

Evangelical writer Rob Bell likes to say that, "If the gospel isn't good news for everybody, then it isn't good news for anybody."

What I want to know is if you believe it's good news for you. Or maybe you hear a little voice whispering: *You're not holy enough, not righteous enough, not good enough.*

None of us deserves God's forgiveness. None of us has earned the right to sit at his table. The good news is that God pulls out a chair anyway. God doesn't play favorites. He loves his children. All of them.

When the great theologian and reformer Martin Luther died, a little note was found in his pocket. The last line read: *We are beggars; this is true.*

It is. That Gentile woman knows it. She knows it so deep in her bones that she believes licking the crumbs off Jesus' floor will be enough. And she is right.

But Jesus doesn't want to toss us crumbs. We might be beggars but what is on offer isn't scraps, but the bread of heaven and the cup of salvation. And it's yours if you want it. It's yours if you're willing to ask. I can only imagine the disciples sitting around the campfire that night as they are beginning to learn that God doesn't pick and choose who to love, which means they can't either. I bet that was a scary revelation. God doesn't play favorites, but we do.

Will Campbell was a Baptist minister from Mississippi who did all sorts of crazy things. For a while, he worked at the University of Mississippi but left because his views on racial equality attracted too many death threats. In 1957, he escorted nine black teenagers into a high school that had never taught black students. He was the only white person at the founding of the Southern Christian Leadership Conference, led by the Rev. Dr. Martin Luther King Jr.

By all accounts, Campbell was doing good work, fighting for the right side. But he was doing more than fighting: He was following Jesus. And you just never know what's going to happen when a person does that.

Campbell began to realize he hated the racial bigots he opposed. He saw how easy it was to take sides and to demonize the other. *Interesting*, he thought, *that God hates all the same people I do.*

So Campbell did something truly crazy. He started sipping whiskey with the Ku Klux Klan. He officiated their weddings and put their bodies in the ground when they died. When they got sick, he emptied their bedpans. Campbell loved these men.

"God doesn't play favorites," Campbell said. "How can I?"

I'm not sure I could follow in Will Campbell's footsteps. I'm not sure my love has evolved that fully yet. I'm not sure it ever will. But *that is* what following Jesus looks like. And I want to follow Jesus. Do you?

You know what helps me to find the will to follow Jesus? Hearing the voice of that humble woman down on her knees. "Yes, Lord, yet even the dogs eat the crumbs that fall from their masters' table."

None of us deserves God's forgiveness. Acknowledging this makes it easier to love people we don't think deserve to be loved. Especially when that person is you or me.

We don't have to earn God's love. We just have to be humble enough to ask for it. At the end of the day, we're all beggars.

I thank God that's enough. I thank God that I'm enough. I thank God that you're enough.

You're enough.

You're enough.

You are enough.

religiously blind

As he walked along, he saw a man blind from birth. His disciples asked him, "Rabbi, who sinned, this man or his parents, that he was born blind?" Jesus answered, "Neither this man nor his parents sinned; he was born blind so that God's works might be revealed in him. We must work the works of him who sent me while it is day; night is coming when no one can work. As long as I am in the world, I am the light of the world." When he had said this, he spat on the ground and made mud with the saliva and spread the mud on the man's eyes, saying to him, "Go, wash in the pool of Siloam" (which means Sent). Then he went and washed and came back able to see.

The neighbors and those who had seen him before as a beggar began to ask, "Is this not the man who used to sit and beg?" Some were saying, "It is he." Others were saying, "No, but it is someone like him." He kept saying, "I am the man." But they kept asking him, "Then how were your eyes opened?" He answered, "The man called Jesus made mud, spread it on my eyes, and said to me, 'Go to Siloam and wash.' Then I went and washed and received my sight." They said to him, "Where is he?" He said, "I do not know."

They brought to the Pharisees the man who had formerly been blind. Now it was a sabbath day when

Jesus made the mud and opened his eyes. Then the Pharisees also began to ask him how he had received his sight. He said to them, "He put mud on my eyes. Then I washed, and now I see." Some of the Pharisees said, "This man is not from God, for he does not observe the sabbath." But others said, "How can a man who is a sinner perform such signs?" And they were divided. So they said again to the blind man, "What do you say about him? It was your eyes he opened."

He said, "He is a prophet." The Jews did not believe that he had been blind and had received his sight until they called the parents of the man who had received his sight and asked them, "Is this your son, who you say was born blind? How then does he now see?" His parents answered, "We know that this is our son, and that he was born blind; but we do not know how it is that now he sees, nor do we know who opened his eyes. Ask him; he is of age. He will speak for himself." His parents said this because they were afraid of the Jews; for the Jews had already agreed that anyone who confessed Jesus to be the Messiah would be put out of the synagogue. Therefore his parents said, "He is of age; ask him." So for the second time they called the man who had been blind, and they said to him, "Give glory to God! We know that this man is a sinner." He answered, "I do not know whether he is a sinner. One thing I do know, that though I was blind, now I see."

They said to him, "What did he do to you? How did he open your eyes?" He answered them, "I have told you already, and you would not listen. Why do you want to hear it again? Do you also want to become his disciples?" Then they reviled him, saying, "You are his disciple, but we are disciples of Moses. We know that God has spoken to Moses, but as for this man, we do not know where he comes from." The man answered, "Here is an astonishing thing! You do not know where he comes from, and yet he opened my eyes. We know that God does not listen to sinners, but he does listen to one who worships him and obeys his will. Never since the world began has it been heard that anyone opened the eyes of a person born blind. If this man were not from God, he could do nothing." They answered him, "You were born entirely in sins, and are you trying to teach us?" And they drove him out.

John 9:1-34

My mother has been a flight attendant for more than two decades. I remember the day she went for the interview because she picked me up after school in a beautiful red dress I had never seen before. After the interview, she found out that the people doing the hiring noticed her immediately and referred to her all day as the "lady in red." She stood out, which was what she was trying to do. She had been a homemaker for years and didn't have a college degree. She was nervous to secure employment, but my father's business was in trouble and four kids in the house needed to be fed and clothed. So she put on her red dress and went for it. And everybody noticed.

But what they didn't see, what they couldn't have known, was that my mother was terrified of flying. But she needed the job so she summoned her courage, put on her red dress, and flew. I love that about her. She has always been willing to do anything for her family. I want to be just like her when I grow up.

Recently a passenger approached her to report another passenger had threatened him. "He said if I leaned my seat back again, he was going to beat the crap out of me." Mom raised an eyebrow. "Do you think he was joking?"

The man shook his head. "No, ma'am."

"Okay," Mom said, "I'll ring the cockpit and let the captain know. We can have law enforcement board the plane when we land."

"No, no," he said. "I don't want to cause a scene. I just wanted you to know. You know…in case something happens to me."

"We won't let that happen. But just to be safe, let's move you to another seat."

Later in the flight, mom was taking drink orders when she arrived at the row where the alleged villain sat. She checked him out and saw that he was well-dressed and appeared to be of sound mind and body. But the passengers around him looked stressed. Apparently, the tension from the earlier confrontation was still very much alive. The villain ordered a ginger ale.

Mom left to retrieve the drinks. When she returned, she realized she had forgotten the ginger ale.

Not good.

She apologized and said she would be right back with his drink.

The passengers winced. But the man surprised everyone by saying, "You know what? Make it a club soda. I forgot." He snapped his fingers. "I gave up ginger ale for Lent."

Mom's jaw hit the floor. I don't want to throw stones at this guy, but we Christians sure do give our religion a bad name. I know I do.

The great pacificist Mahatma Gandhi said, "I like Christ, just not Christians. They're so unlike Christ." Ouch. I've tried to let that quote challenge me as opposed to offending me. When people want to know if what they read about Jesus is true, they often look to the lives of those who profess him as Lord. I think about that. Let that sink in.

When I was a kid, someone once told me to behave because I might be the only Jesus someone ever saw. I thought, *That's really too bad.* But seriously, when we—the religious—turn people off from Jesus, that's a problem. A popular mantra of my generation is that "we're spiritual but not religious." This is another way of saying "we're open to God but suspect of his people." I imagine this sentiment would ring true with the beggar from our lesson. Blind since birth, he encounters Jesus, who takes dirt, spits in it, and anoints the man's face with the mud. For the first time in his life, the blind man moves from dark to light. But then he runs into a bunch of religious folks, and things go sideways.

Before he's even healed, the disciples point at him and say, "Rabbi, who sinned, this man or his parents, that he was born blind?"

It was a commonly held belief in the ancient world that illness and disability were direct results of sin. But Jesus will hear nothing of that kind of insane talk. *Nobody sinned,* he says. *Come on. You're smarter than that. This man is who he is, as you are who you are. He's a person, fully formed, in whom the work of God will be made manifest.*

On a recent evening I was running at my neighborhood track when I saw a severely disabled teenager using a walker in the lane next to me. His father was a few paces ahead but keeping an eye on his son. As I ran by, I became hyper aware of my able body. I felt guilty for running with such ease while this teenager fought hard for every step he took.

On the next lap, I got a better look at the teen's face. It was painted in joy. He was smiling—radiant and happy to be walking in the cool of the evening with his father. And I thought, *How dare I marginalize this young man? How dare I presume to know anything about him?*

Two thousand years ago we see Jesus looking at the disabled and declaring them full people in every sense of the word. The disciples' question has to do with exclusion. They want to know who is responsible for keeping the blind beggar shut out from society.

Jesus replies by saying, *Wrong question. No one is excluded. I am the light of the world, and my light shines on all people. All people.*

After the beggar's encounter with Jesus, his neighbors drag him before the Pharisees to give an account for his healing. And like our villain on the plane who gave up ginger ale for Lent, they make a mess of religion. They simply don't believe the story of the formerly blind man.

They badger him and question his integrity. They haul his parents in to testify as to whether or not he was actually even blind. They call Jesus a sinner and say the healed man is nothing more than a disciple of a sinner.

The beggar fights back. *Look, I don't know who he is; I haven't a clue if Jesus is a sinner. But if he were not from God, how could he open my eyes? I was blind, but now I see.*

That does it. The Pharisees eject the man from the synagogue, asking, "You were born entirely in sins, and are you trying to teach us?"

With those words, we reach the heart of the story: blindness, but not of the eyes. This is a blindness of the spirit. Physical blindness, challenging as it may be, only has so much power. Our physical condition never speaks of our true identity. Our physical conditions are constantly shifting, sometimes for better and other times for worse.

God is far more interested in what is on the inside than on the outside. God does not see as mortals do. God does not look upon outward appearances. God looks upon our hearts (1 Samuel 16:7).

This makes spiritual blindness a serious issue. When our spirits are blind, we no can no longer see the works of God, not even when they are brought and laid before us. The Pharisees are certain they know how God works and how God doesn't. So when Jesus heals this man on the Sabbath, it can't be from God, because God doesn't work this way.

The Pharisees take it on the chin a lot. They're a favorite punching bag for many Christians. But you know what? They are just trying to be faithful—or at least faithful in the way they understand it. Sure, they are obsessed with religious rules, but their obsession comes from a good place. They are trying to be devoted to God. But in this instance (and others), their religious devotion blinds them.

This reality should terrify us. How can we ever know if we are seeing correctly or not? Dan Clendenin, founder of the Journey with Jesus webzine, says, "One of the most dangerous spiritual places we can live is in the deluded notion that we are a fully sighted person."

There's something to that. Think of Westboro Baptist Church—infamous for protesting funerals of American soldiers and rallying against all kinds of people and communities. I've often wondered what drives people to such extremes. They must have a deep-rooted belief that they see the world rightly. The man on my mother's flight saw no contradiction between threatening a fellow passenger's life and touting religious devotion. His bad behavior may be obvious to us, but it wasn't to him. And remember: by all outward appearances, this man had it together.

None of us are fully sighted people. We will at times behave in ways that are not only unfaithful, but egregiously so. It's easy to get into trouble when we think we've got life all figured out. We may not spout hate speech at the funeral of a war hero or frighten the folks sitting near us on airplanes, but we have our notions about right and wrong. Why consult God in prayer? We know who to vote for so why do we need to listen to another person's perspective? We know what's good and bad in this world so why bother reading scripture?

We know. We know. We know.

I wish I identified with the blind beggar in this story—a man who knows he is blind and can thus recognize the light. Maybe some days I do see the light. But more often than not, I'm the Pharisee, believing I can see, when in reality I cannot.

Do you know what I have discovered? The healthiest people don't just admit their blindness—they embrace it. The wise person readily admits, "I don't know. I don't know. I don't know."

Long ago, a newspaper posed the question, "What's Wrong with the World?" The great writer G.K. Chesterton wrote back, "Dear Sirs: I am."

If we hope to see the light, we must acknowledge we are in the dark. The first step in any recovery process is admitting there's a problem. Jesus does not come for the healthy but the sick. A healthy person doesn't need a doctor. A sick person does. The righteous can keep on being righteous, but sinners? Well, we need a savior.

During the past few years, the most visible Christian in the world has garnered unprecedented attention. Pope Francis has been called a rock-star pope—a title he finds offensive. I thought this was kind of awesome. Most people dream of being seen as a rock star! Not

Pope Francis. He has spent his entire priestly ministry living with and serving the poor. Despite his tremendous wealth as Pope, he cooks his own meals and eschews the papal apartment, choosing instead to live in a humble Vatican guesthouse. Before he was elected Pope, Francis drove himself around instead of relying on a chaffeur. Once elected, he turned in the papal Mercedes in favor of a five-year-old Ford Focus.

Pope Francis hasn't changed any doctrines of the Roman Catholic Church. He hasn't overwhelmed anyone with electric preaching—he is not youthful or handsome. He's not even considered a great theologian by most people. And yet Francis is setting the world on fire with his talk of God. I have atheist friends who despise religion but like this pope! What's up with that?

Maybe it's because Francis is real. I love a story that I heard about him. While he was burying the priest who had been his confessor years earlier, he stole a rosary from the casket. Pope Francis said it took a little work to pry it from the priest's cold fingers, but he got the job done. Then Pope Francis asked the priest to forgive him one last time. How awesome is that? A funny pope. Who knew?

On another occasion, a reporter asked him, "Who are you?" Pope Francis sat in silence for a moment and then answered, "I am a sinner. A sinner whom the Lord has looked upon."

Humility is a warm light that draws all people toward it. Proverbs declares that the fear of the Lord is the beginning of wisdom. If we hope to see, we must first understand that we are blind. Because of the grace and great love of our Lord, we have not been left to stumble in the dark: The light of Christ shines on all people—on popes and beggars, saints and sinners, you and me.

How do we know if we are seeing the light?

I don't know, the beggar said to the Pharisees. *I don't have all the answers. But one thing I know: Jesus touched my eyes. And where once I was blind, now I see.*

just
drink
the wine

Meanwhile the disciples were urging him, "Rabbi, eat something." But he said to them, "I have food to eat that you do not know about." So the disciples said to one another, "Surely no one has brought him something to eat?"

John 4:31-33

I spent a summer in Dijon, France, trying to learn the most beautiful of languages. The night I arrived was like many travelers' experiences of landing in a foreign country—it was late, and I was tired. All I wanted to do was go to sleep.

But this is not how the French do things. My host family had prepared an elaborate meal, a meal they were waiting to enjoy until I arrived.

Let me give you a little backstory. Normally students at my college didn't make this trip until they had been studying French for at least two years. I had one semester under my belt—I literally knew nothing. To this day, I don't know why the department head allowed me to go. She called me *la bebe* of the group. And then she would laugh. I think she enjoyed listening to my horrible, Texan-accented French.

My host family hadn't gotten the memo about my nascent studies. So I arrived, sat down at the table, and the French started flying. I did my best. I really tried. I smiled...I fake laughed... I nodded...I said... *Bonjour!* A lot.

After a few minutes the father stood up and made an elaborate show of bringing out a bottle of wine. Even with my elementary knowledge of French, I quickly realized this was no standard bottle of wine. It had been saved for a special occasion, and the father carried it to the table with the care of a man presenting his newborn child. *Behold this!*

So the family watched with bated breath as the bottle was uncorked— slowly and deliberately. The father took my glass and poured the wine as if I were a king and he my humble servant. And then all eyes in the room fell on me. The table was set. The food was ready. And now, the guest of honor was in his seat. The dinner would not proceed until I tasted the wine.

Here's my inner monologue. *I'm only 19. I don't drink wine. I'm not supposed to drink wine. I have never had a single glass of wine in my life. But I'm in France. I can drink wine in France. Right? I should drink wine in France. So let him pour the wine. No! Don't you dare let him pour the wine! You're a good Baptist. Don't let the French corrupt you. Not on the first night!*

I reached for the glass, but I didn't pick it up. I waved it off. "*Non, merci,*" I said and asked for a Coke instead. The ghastly look on the father's face haunts me to this day. He wasn't offended. He wasn't angry. It was something far worse than that. He was hurt. He had offered me his very best wine, and I had refused it. Why? Because I didn't know what I was missing.

This is where we find the disciples in our lesson. Jesus has been working and the disciples are worried about him. *Rabbi,* they say. *You need to eat something.*

I'm fine, he replies. "I have food to eat that you do not know about."

They look at each other, wondering what he can possibly mean? *Did you bring him food?* someone asks. *I didn't bring him food,* another answers. *Then who brought him food?*

My food, Jesus says, *is to do the will of him who sent me and to accomplish his work.*

My food, Jesus says. *My* food.

What is *your* food?

I have always wondered about Jesus and food. What did he like to eat? Did he spill food on his shirt like I often do or did he eat slowly and politely like my grandmother? How much wine did he actually drink? And what was Happy Hour Jesus like? How did he go without food for forty days at the start of his ministry?

In the Sermon on the Mount, Jesus speaks of fasting just after he teaches the disciples to pray and suggests that fasting be as common an affair as prayer. He isn't so much commanding us to follow this practice as assuming we will. And the early Christians do. If a church member was hungry, it was common for the entire community to go without until they could provide for their brother or sister in need. Fasting has been an important part of Christianity from the very beginning.

But the early Christians didn't just fast for the sake of others; they fasted because they understood it was good for them. It revealed their frailty.

Allow me to explain. *Do you consider yourself a strong and patient person?*

Yes? Okay, strong and patient person, skip a meal. Then skip another one. Skip three. Don't eat for an entire day. How mentally and emotionally strong do you feel after a full day of no food?

Fasting strips away the illusion that we sustain ourselves. It brings our frailty acutely to mind. Hunger brings us to our knees in a way not much else in life can. And that can be helpful.

But can I be honest with you? I don't like fasting. Actually, that's not true. I hate fasting. I hate it because fasting is hard.

If you don't eat enough, you get weak. If you don't eat right, you get sick. If you don't eat at all, you get me.

I told a friend recently that I can almost bench press my body weight. "Really?" he asked. "All 75 pounds?"

It made me laugh. But the truth is I've been wildly self-conscious about my weight my entire life. I'm a really skinny guy. When I was in junior high, I fantasized about the muscles that would someday come. *Just a year or two more,* I would think, *and I'll start to fill out. It won't be long before I'll rip off my shirt at the pool and impress all the ladies.*

That day never came. I could spend the next year of my life doing nothing but lifting weights, and it wouldn't make much difference. I'm just a skinny guy—it's who I am.

You're something else. You may be skinny. You may be fat. You may be short or tall or ready to be on the cover of a fitness magazine. I have no idea what you look like, but I do know something about you. I know food plays a big role in your self-esteem. You either want to eat more of it, or you're dying to eat less. Either way, whenever you look in the mirror, you think about food.

Food is really hard. And body image is only the start of it.

When I went to college, I knew no one. I did not have a single friend on campus, which made the first week tough—especially during mealtime. I dreaded going to the cafeteria and eating alone. Ever been there?

So one night I'm in line and a pretty girl who I had never seen before looks at me and says, "Oh my gosh! Oh my gosh! Oh my gosh!"

"What?" I said, shocked that she was talking to me.

"I cannot believe this!" she screamed.

"What?!" *You wanna marry me?*

"We. Are. Wearing. The *same* sweatpants!"

The world stopped spinning. I looked down at my pants. Yep. I had stolen them from my sister before I left for school. They were brand name—Abercrombie & Fitch—and I thought they looked cool. I also thought nobody would know they were made for girls. I was wrong.

"We have to get a picture," she said. "We just have to. Hold on. Let me get my boyfriend." She turned around and yelled across the cafeteria. "Mark! Mark! Get over here!" Mark came over, took our picture, and then I ate dinner. Alone.

Loneliness can make food hard. So can our doctors when they tell us our cholesterol isn't what it should be. Or the budget tightens up, and we have to stop eating out. Food is wonderful, but food is hard, complicated, and inescapable.

This is why the disciples worry about Jesus. A brother needs to eat. But Jesus says to them, "My food is to do the will of him who sent me, and to accomplish his work."

I guarantee Peter rolls his eyes at this. It is a bit holier than thou, if I may say so.

One night in college I drove a friend home in a sports car my parents had given me. He said, "Yeah, my parents gave me a Mustang GT for graduation."

"Sweet," I said. "You'll have to give me a ride sometime."

"Not possible," he said.

"Why not?"

"I gave it back. Driving a car like that was making me prideful." He thumped his fingers on my dashboard. "I decided I didn't need the temptation. I genuinely want to be like Jesus."

Awkward.

Is this what Jesus is doing in our lesson? Is he shaming his disciples for wanting to eat? I don't think so. Jesus isn't too holy to eat. It's just that food isn't the *only* thing he eats. He knows of another food—one that satisfies not the stomach but the soul, a table that serves not bread, but love and mercy and a peace that passes all understanding.

Do you know *that* food?

That food saved my life. I have learned that I can have it all—rich food, fine wine, but it's never enough. I need more than to feed my body. I need to have my soul saved. And there's only one table in the world serving that food.

Jesus isn't shaming the disciples. He is being honest about what sustains him, and he wants them to know so they can eat it too. "My food…" he says "can be *your* food."

Dallas Willard was a philosopher and mystic who wrote a lot about fasting. Dallas said he would fast whenever he got tired or stressed. When he hit a valley, he fasted. Not me. For me, fasting tends to happen when I'm in a good place, when I'm feeling holy and strong and ready. But Dallas fasted when he felt weak.

Why?

Because when life gets shaky, we reach for that which steadies us. We reach for our food, whatever that substance may be.

What's *your* food?

TV? Exercise? Work? Sex?

None of these are bad. But none of them will feed your soul like God. Dallas understood this. He said it took years of practice, but eventually he came to a point where fasting allowed God's energy to flow through him in ways he never thought possible. The energy he drew from God calmed him and sustained him like food or drink never could. "Man does not live by bread alone," Jesus told Satan, "but the very Word of God." Dallas ate *that* food.

I've been feeling frail lately. And while I've undergone no great fast, I've tried to feed on God in a very specific way. I've been praying the Jesus Prayer. Do you know it? It goes like this: *Jesus Christ, Son of God, have mercy on me a sinner.* When I'm tired or frustrated or anxious or hungry, I pray those words over and over and over again. I *eat* those words as if my life depended on them, which, of course, it does. And I'm telling you…God transforms my frailty into strength. I cannot explain it. I only know that this happens.

A lot of people think fasting is about testing our faith. That misses the point. Fasting isn't about *not* eating; it's about eating something *else*. But you can't eat if you're already full. And so the question you have to ask yourself is: Do I have room for what Jesus eats? Am I willing to fast so I might be filled?

Dallas died last year. He had cancer, and he knew it was the end. He was cleaning out his office with his friend John, when out of the blue Dallas said, "John? I think that when I die, it might be some time before I know it."[1]

No one can say for sure what Dallas meant by those words, but I have an idea. Dallas spent serious time with Jesus. He feasted on the Lord. He ate the bread of heaven and drank from the cup of salvation, and because of that he was filled with God. So much so that crossing from this life into the next seemed to him a most natural thing to do.

Most of us have no idea what we're missing. There is food of which this world does not know. But will we eat it?

This food isn't just for the Dallas Willards of the world—it is for you and for me.

Sometimes I dream I'm back in France on that first night, and the father offers me his wine. But in my dream, I don't refuse the cup. Instead, I drink deeply from it, trusting that what the father offers is precisely what I need.

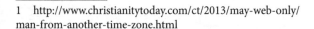

1 http://www.christianitytoday.com/ct/2013/may-web-only/man-from-another-time-zone.html

just
say
yes

In the sixth month the angel Gabriel was sent by God to a town in Galilee called Nazareth, to a virgin engaged to a man whose name was Joseph, of the house of David. The virgin's name was Mary. And he came to her and said, "Greetings, favored one! The Lord is with you." But she was much perplexed by his words and pondered what sort of greeting this might be. The angel said to her, "Do not be afraid, Mary, for you have found favor with God. And now, you will conceive in your womb and bear a son, and you will name him Jesus. He will be great, and will be called the Son of the Most High, and the Lord God will give to him the throne of his ancestor David. He will reign over the house of Jacob forever, and of his kingdom there will be no end." Mary said to the angel, "How can this be, since I am a virgin?" The angel said to her, "The Holy Spirit will come upon you, and the power of the Most High will overshadow you; therefore the child to be born will be holy; he will be called Son of God. And now, your relative Elizabeth in her old age has also conceived a son; and this is the sixth month for her who was said to be barren. For nothing will be impossible with God." Then Mary said, "Here am I, the servant of the Lord; let it be with me according to your word." Then the angel departed from her.

Luke 1:26-38

I have loved the Bible for as long as I can remember. I was never one of those kids who had to be coerced into reading it. I just did it. But don't get the wrong impression about me—there was no actual piety involved. I just liked how wild the Bible was.

On every other page, somebody was starting a war or stealing treasure or being miraculously saved from hungry lions. It was totally wheels-off, better than anything I was allowed to watch on television. I used to think, *My parents must not know what's in here... because if they did, there's no way they would allow me to read it.*

And that's saying nothing of the more—how shall I put it?—sensual passages. I used to sneak a Bible into my bed at night and read Proverbs 5:19 over and over again. "A loving doe, a graceful deer, may her breasts satisfy you always, may you ever be intoxicated with her love." *Whoa. Breasts! The Bible talks about breasts.* I nearly lost my mind when I discovered the Song of Songs.

So I read the Bible—but not always for the most sacred reasons. That's not to say I didn't believe or respect it—I did. I found the story of Jesus Christ so hauntingly beautiful that it simply had to be true. I was drawn to the idea that God wasn't satisfied to stay in the heavens, far removed from his beloved creatures, so he did the unthinkable: God became one of us so we might know of God's love. If *that* were true, I thought, then *anything* was possible. I liked this idea. After all, what could be more impossible than the incarnation?

Still, my love affair with scripture hit a snag the day I realized I wasn't in the Bible—and never would be. Here were all these amazing stories about God's favorite people in the ancient world doing amazing things. And there I was in the 1980s, *reading* all about it. Adam and Eve may have screwed up, but at least they were invited to the party.

I took this existential crisis to my father. "Dad, is the Bible finished?"

"What do you mean?"

"Like, is it over? Has it all been written?"

"Yeah, it's over," he said.

"You're sure it's not a rough draft? Like, maybe we do something great, then our story gets tacked on to the end?"

He shook his head no.

I was crushed, jealous of folks like Mary. There she was, so young (barely fifteen!) living in a nothing town, betrothed to some nothing guy, when all the sudden she's thrust right into the heart of God's story. The angel Gabriel appears and announces God's unimaginable decision to become human. But to do so, he must first become a child. And to do *that,* he needs Mary's help.

Can you imagine God needing *your* help?

Greetings, favored one! Gabriel says. *The Lord is with you. Do not be afraid, God favors you. You'll conceive and bear a son, and name him Jesus. He'll be great and will reign over the house of Jacob forever, and of his kingdom there will be no end.*

How can this be? Mary says. *I'm a virgin.*

The Holy Spirit will overshadow you. For nothing is impossible with God.

Right on, she says. *Here I am, the servant of the Lord; let it be with me according to your word.*

And with her reply, Gabriel leaves.

The scene is fast, the language sparse. Mary's concern is followed so closely by her obedience that we barely even notice it. But that would be missing the point. This isn't some tranquil exchange between a flowery angel and an obedient little girl.

This is a terrifying episode. It also isn't the plan. And this is critically important.

Mary is betrothed to Joseph. Ancient betrothals aren't like modern engagements. Joseph hasn't spent a year wooing Mary with candlelit dinners and red wine. This marriage has been arranged with little to no consideration for what Mary thinks or feels. Her job is to present herself as a virgin for Joseph. End of story. Turning up pregnant is about the worst thing she can do. In the best-case scenario, Mary can expect to be abandoned by Joseph and treated as a pariah in the community. At worst, she will be killed, most likely by a public stoning.

You're to have a son, Gabriel says. *Soon. Before your wedding.* Let these words hit you like they did Mary. Don't skip ahead to Christmas. Don't see Joseph at Mary's side while she holds the hope of the world in her arms. Don't see heaven and earth rejoicing at the birth of a Savior. Mary sees none of that. For us to understand the full story, we can't either. All Mary sees is an angel asking her to put everything—her reputation, her marriage, her very life—on the line.

Enter her confusion. Feel her fear.

The angel tells her she is to be *Theotokos*—"the God bearer"—the one to carry in her womb, give birth to, nurse, and raise the *only* Son of God. Allow the weight of this impossible request to settle upon your shoulders.

For years I've tried to imagine Mary. Sometimes I picture this girl living in a dangerous world brandishing a kind of courage I'll never even catch a sniff. Other times, I have conjured her as a simple, obedient girl who does exactly what the angel asks of her.

Deep down, I knew neither of these images did justice to the real Mary. I wanted to see the face of a girl so brave she is willing to say yes to the impossible. And then, a few years ago, I finally did.

She appeared on my television. Her name wasn't Mary, but it was close: Malala. She had brown skin, jet-black hair, and eyes that emitted fierce love. Malala had just been shot. She was fifteen years old and, like Mary, lived in a land with grave consequences for girls who try the impossible.

Malala's Pakistani town had once been a draw for tourists before the Taliban arrived and imposed Sharia law. Malala, however, had been publicly speaking against the Taliban since she was ten years old. *Ten.*

And what was the cause so dear that she was willing to risk her life? Education. Malala dared to believe that young girls in Pakistan deserved the right to go to school. And for that, evil men tried to snuff out her life.

But Malala survived, and her voice grew louder, even as her life remained in danger. She has never backed down. In the years since the attack, Malala has continued to do and *be* the impossible. She's a teenage girl fighting terrorism with her voice, combating evil with love, and inspiring millions to do the same.

In 2014 Malala became the youngest person to receive the Nobel Peace Prize. Malala said, "I had two options—one was to remain silent and wait to be killed. And the second was to speak up and then be killed. I chose the second one. I decided to speak up."[1]

As I heard those words, I thought, *There! That's the reality Mary faced. A lose-lose situation. Say yes to God and face death. Or say no to God and face the spiritual death of having refused God.*

You're to have a son, Mary, Gabriel says. *The Son of the Most High, conceived by the Holy Spirit.*

You know what's really interesting? Gabriel doesn't ask for Mary's permission. He *tells* her it will happen. This is a lot like our lives, isn't it? We make our plans. Then life happens. And it's not what we planned. Sometimes it's just the opposite. Sometimes terrible things happen.

I think about the mass shooting at Sandy Hook Elementary School in Newtown, Connecticut. It's been a few years since we lost those young children and their teachers. As I have with Mary and Malala, I marvel at the parents who have dedicated their lives to preventing such future tragedies while enduring their own.

The evening of the shooting, a priest in Newtown said some of his parishioners asked if they ought to turn off their Christmas lights. *Should we, given what's happened, turn off our lights?* It was a good question. I probably would have turned mine off. I don't know how to celebrate when children are taken from parents. I don't. If my child had been killed at school, I would have done more than turn off my Christmas lights.

But the priest said no. "We don't turn off our Christmas lights," he said, "because we can't lose hope."

---

1   https://www.nobelprize.org/nobel_prizes/peace/laureates/2014/yousafzai-lecture_en.html

He's right. Saint John says it this way: "The light shines in the darkness and the darkness has not overcome it."

We don't choose the circumstances of our lives. Mary didn't. Malala didn't. Newtown didn't.

In life, good things and terrible things will happen. We can't control them. What we can control is whether we keep the light on in our hearts. Will we say yes or no to God? Our answer is just about the only thing in this life we can control. Gabriel does not ask Mary's permission. But she still has a choice, the same one we have. She can resist, fight back, make excuses—just like we can when God asks us to bear Jesus into the world.

But Mary asks one reasonable question, is given an unreasonable answer, and still says yes.

Is it reasonable to believe in a virgin birth? Of course not. But miracles are rarely reasonable. They are something entirely better than reasonable. They're true.

I can't say for sure why Mary goes along with God's plan. But I have a hunch. She trusts Gabriel when he says that with God, nothing is impossible. This assurance doesn't take away her fear or explain how everything will work out. But it allows her to speak this one glorious line: "Behold, I am the handmaid of the Lord; let it be to me according to your word."

The question for us today is whether we will say *yes, let it be to me according to your word*. Thirteenth-century mystic and theologian Meister Eckhart said, "We are all meant to be mothers of God."

If that's true, it means I made it into the Bible after all. So have you. The Bible is never really finished. Our names may not appear on the pages but our lives are woven into it every time we say yes to God.

When you hear Gabriel tell Mary the Lord is with her, know the Lord is also with you. And when your moment comes to trust God and believe in the impossible, say yes. Terrible things will happen, and so will miracles.

poor gus

"Then the kingdom of heaven will be like this. Ten bridesmaids took their lamps and went to meet the bridegroom. Five of them were foolish, and five were wise. When the foolish took their lamps, they took no oil with them; but the wise took flasks of oil with their lamps. As the bridegroom was delayed, all of them became drowsy and slept. But at midnight there was a shout, 'Look! Here is the bridegroom! Come out to meet him.' Then all those bridesmaids got up and trimmed their lamps. The foolish said to the wise, 'Give us some of your oil, for our lamps are going out.' But the wise replied, 'No! there will not be enough for you and for us; you had better go to the dealers and buy some for yourselves.' And while they went to buy it, the bridegroom came, and those who were ready went with him into the wedding banquet; and the door was shut. Later the other bridesmaids came also, saying, 'Lord, lord, open to us.' But he replied, 'Truly I tell you, I do not know you.' Keep awake therefore, for you know neither the day nor the hour.

Matthew 25:1-13

A few years ago, I signed up for a weekend course to earn a motorcycle license. I didn't own a bike, but my father did, and I thought it would be fun to ride his occasionally. What wasn't fun was my drill sergeant instructor. She was a little woman with hard eyes; a cigarette dangled permanently from her bottom lip. She ate lunch with it there. I don't know how she did that.

There were three soldiers in the class, recently home from war, and even they were scared of her. Another guy in the class was Gus, a sweet, mild-mannered truck driver who had taken the weekend off work to complete the course. Gus told us that his lifelong dream was to get his license, buy a Harley, and tour the country with his wife. This course was a big deal for Gus.

As the weekend continued, we learned various maneuvers. Gus struggled to learn and keep up. The barking of our drill sergeant didn't help. She sniffed out Gus' weaknesses immediately. Then she pressed on them.

Gus was cautious and focused, but no matter how hard he tried, he just couldn't handle the bike. But he didn't give up. Gus kept working, kept listening, kept trying. And he did improve…kind of.

At the end of the weekend, when all the riding was done, our instructor told us to circle up. "Everyone but Gus," she said. "Gus," she pointed to a tree, "go stand over there."

Gus shuffled away. Our instructor then addressed those of us inside the circle: "Grab the person's hand next to you and raise it up. Congratulations!" she hollered. "You passed!"

I looked over at Gus. His head was down, humiliated, no doubt thinking about telling his wife he had failed, that the hours he had missed from work and the money he'd spent had all been for nothing. It made me sad to see him standing outside the circle.

And then it made me mad. Why was the instructor making such a spectacle of Gus? She had to pass or fail Gus—I get that—but she could have done it differently. I could have too. I could have said something. I *should* have said something. I should have at least told Gus I was sorry—that I wished it had gone differently. Instead, I left as quickly as I could, avoiding eye contact with Gus the whole way. I felt badly for him, no doubt, but I also felt relieved to be included in the circle.

I feel the same emotions when I read the parable of the ten bridesmaids. Jesus says the kingdom of heaven is like ten bridesmaids waiting for a bridegroom. Five are wise, and five aren't. The wise ones bring enough oil to keep their lamps lit in case the bridegroom is delayed. The foolish do not. So when the bridegroom finally arrives, and the foolish are found unprepared, they're shut out from the celebration.

On one hand, I'm relieved to know that if we ready ourselves for the coming of Christ (the bridegroom), then we (the bridesmaids) will be with him. But on the other hand, I feel badly for the foolish bridesmaids standing in the dark.

Lord! Lord, open up! they cry.

But the bridegroom replies, *I don't know you.*

The bridegroom seems cruel to me. Why can't the foolish bridesmaids come in? Because they ran out of oil? Big deal. Who seriously cares? Are we not allowed to make any mistakes when it comes to God? The wise ones aren't perfect either. They all fell asleep!

This is a bizarre parable, one that I honestly don't like. I'm probably not supposed to say that about a story in the Bible. But have you ever felt that way too? Opened the Bible only to discover you didn't like what you found there? I mean, it's a big book with lots of words to love and ponder. But there are also a lot of words that make me super uncomfortable. There are passages that tell women to be silent in church, passages that describe homosexuals as abominations, and passages where God orders the destruction of women and children in war. These passages used to turn me away from the Bible. At one point in my life, they almost made me walk away from the Bible completely. I wanted my Bible to be clear and simple. I wanted it to point me in the right direction, to give me certainty about my life—without complicated and hard-to-understand (and harder-to-implement) lessons.

Then I experienced real life and learned that real life is anything but clear and simple. Slowly but surely, the messy Bible became attractive to me, reflecting what I knew to be true about life. Life—and the words of scripture—are hard and messy and confusing. The Bible isn't meant to make us feel good; it's meant to lead us to God and fill us with truth. And sometimes truth is hard to hear.

The Bible—like Jesus—will comfort us, no doubt about it. But the Bible will also poke and prod us. And if we're wise, we'll let it. If we don't, we rob the Bible of its power. You can find a feel-good message of your choosing with a quick Google search. But truth? Truth that imparts actual wisdom? This is much harder to find. Don't feel badly when the Bible frustrates you. Don't shut the book, close up shop, and move on to another guide for faith or life. Being frustrated by the Bible probably means you're actually reading the thing.

This parable about the ten bridesmaids is an excellent case in point. Who wants to read about a bunch of women calling upon God and God and refusing to answer? It's tempting to skip this story and pretend it doesn't exist. But we do so at our own peril because if we believe that all scripture comes from God, we must trust that *all* scripture carries messages from God—messages God needs us to hear.

One of these hard-to-hear messages is that there is a side of Jesus we have not yet seen. As Christians we believe that Christ has died, Christ has risen, and that Christ will come again. This effectively means we live in tension, having already experienced Jesus but also knowing there's another side to him—that of judge.

The Gospel of Matthew goes to great pains to make this clear. John the Baptist says: "I baptize you with water for repentance, but one who is more powerful than I is coming after me; I am not worthy to carry his sandals. He will baptize you with the Holy Spirit and fire. His winnowing fork is in his hand, and he will clear his threshing floor and will gather his wheat into the granary; but the chaff he will burn with unquenchable fire" (3:11-12).

Yowzers. In other words, the brother is coming back. And when Jesus comes back, some kind of judgment is going to be exacted. We are going to have to answer for the manners in which we lived our lives. What will this look like exactly? Who can say? All we know is that some kind of accounting will take place. *Gulp.*

An easy treatment of this passage would be to view it as only a picture of judgment: Jesus returns, some are saved, and some aren't. Sheep go to heaven, and goats go to hell. That kind of judgment may, in the end, be what happens. This is what the church has taught. Further, some people want nothing to do with God. The hard truth is that they may never change. Who knows how this judgment will end up for them? Thankfully it's not our job to judge.

Yet this one-dimensional understanding of the parable of the ten bridesmaids doesn't quite mesh with the actions of Jesus. If we're talking about the church, then yes, the church shuts its doors all the time. Sadly, the *church* loves to shut its doors. So do I. And so do you. I pulled up to a stoplight the other day and saw a panhandler coming toward my car. Do you know what I did? I locked my door and pretended to look at something urgent on my phone.

Jesus Christ does not live like this. He doesn't shut his doors. Ever. His life is spent opening all the doors he possibly can, especially the ones that are supposed to be kept locked.

Lepers. Bandits. Prostitutes. Gentiles. Sinners. These people society judges as on the wrong side of the door become some of Jesus' closest friends. These are the people to whom he declares the door no longer exists: He has *become* the door. And in him, they are free to walk through any door. So what is really going on in this lesson? Why doesn't the bridegroom open the door?

Let's put the story into context. When Matthew writes his Gospel, almost an entire generation has passed since Jesus' ascension. That means the eyewitnesses to his life are dying off.

But Jesus has promised to come back *soon*. And now there seems to have been a delay. *Where is he?* They need him. Things aren't going well. The Jews are scattered, and the temple has been destroyed.

His delay must have stirred up some doubt about the whole Jesus movement. We've all been there—lying on our beds, overwhelmed, scared, depressed, begging God to come—and yet…Jesus delays.

I was talking with a teenage girl who had been through some tough stuff. She had the scars on her wrists to prove it. She said, "I try to pray. I want to know God. But when I pray, nothing happens."

"But you still pray?" I asked.

"Yeah," she said softly. "I pray, but I don't expect anything from God anymore."

I don't expect anything anymore. Are there any sadder words?

This a rough place to be, and it's precisely the place Matthew is addressing. This parable isn't just about judgment—it's about a promise of Christ's return. But we don't know when, which means we can do one of two things: Get ready or stop expecting.

This is the only difference between the wise and foolish bridesmaids. The wise aren't more righteous or holy; they are ready for the delay, while the others aren't. That's it.

Are we ready? If Jesus came back today, would he find our lives ready for him to enter? Or would we scramble to get our stuff together?

The longer I meditate on this story, the more I think the bridegroom doesn't keep the door shut because he wants to. The bridegroom *wants* to open the door, desperately. The only reason he keeps it shut is because the bridesmaids aren't ready.

He doesn't say: *I don't like you,* or *I don't forgive you,* or *I don't love you.* He says the saddest words God could ever utter: *I don't know you. I don't know you. You're not ready for me.*

Are we ready? Are you ready? Am I?

Honestly, I don't know. How can we ever know if we're ready for anything until it actually happens? Perhaps a better question to ask is this: Are we *trying* to be ready? Will we *try* to be ready today?

Maybe you want to try but you're not sure what to do. I'll tell you— it's simple. Do that thing you've been meaning to do. You know, that thing God's been whispering about in your ear. I don't know what it is—but you know. Yesterday is gone, and tomorrow may never come. We have today, and that's it. Want to be ready for God? Live by faith today. That's all we can do. That's all we need to do.

> *Call that friend and tell her you're sorry.*
>
> *Sit down and write that letter to your father, thanking him for his love.*
>
> *Make that appointment with the therapist.*

Turn off the TV.

Log off Facebook.

Kiss your partner.

Open your Bible.

Light a candle.

Do something kind.

Make today the day you ready yourself for Jesus' arrival.

It turned out my motorcycle instructor was a bad judge of skill. Hours after receiving my license, I crashed my father's motorcycle. The bike had a sidecar, and I managed to flip the darn thing upside down.

Yep. I was young, reckless, and nowhere near ready to ride that bike. As I was lying stunned on the ground, I thought about Gus. I thought about how he would never have done what I had. He was cautious. He would have been careful. He wouldn't have tried something he wasn't ready for.

Gus had the right heart, if not the right skill. That should have counted for something with our instructor, but it didn't.

The good news is that Jesus Christ doesn't judge like that. It's not our performance that matters most to God; it's the willingness to be ready. God does not see as we see. We look upon outward appearances. But God looks upon our heart.

The bridegroom *is coming.* May today be the day he looks upon your heart and says the most marvelous words God could ever utter.

I know you. I know you.

You're ready.

shielded

Put on the whole armor of God, so that you may
be able to stand against the wiles of the devil.
For our struggle is not against enemies of blood
and flesh, but against the rulers, against the
authorities, against the cosmic powers of this
present darkness, against the spiritual forces of
evil in the heavenly places. Therefore take up
the whole armor of God, so that you may be
able to withstand on that evil day, and having
done everything, to stand firm. Stand therefore,
and fasten the belt of truth around your waist,
and put on the breastplate of righteousness. As
shoes for your feet put on whatever will make
you ready to proclaim the gospel of peace. With
all of these, take the shield of faith, with which
you will be able to quench all the flaming arrows
of the evil one.

Ephesians 6:11-16

I have never carried a shield or been in a situation
where I needed one. This is probably something you
and I have in common. But maybe you are a soldier or
a police officer or someone who knows what it's like
to need a shield. Maybe you know what it's like to be
attacked, to come face to face with an enemy.

I recently heard a photojournalist on public radio describe how it felt to receive an email requesting the exact number of inches between her navel and her breasts. She was heading to Iraq, and a company needed the dimensions to make her body armor. Can you imagine receiving such an email? Can you imagine *replying?*

To need armor to protect you from a bullet or a violent mob is a heightened kind of reality, one I will probably (hopefully) never understand.

But I know how it feels to be protected—most of us do. The click of a lock at night, the warmth of a heavy coat in winter, the embrace of a parent. What a blessing it is to be protected, right?

We know insecurity too. The savings account runs dry, but the bills keep coming. The tumor is back, and it's bigger. The one phone call we really need—the one that could save our marriage—doesn't come.

Protection: We all need it. We all seek it. But we don't all find it.

When I was thirteen, I had night terrors. I would wake up in the dead of the night and run around the house—half-awake, half-naked, wholly terrified and fully believing that the dreams were real.

The first time it happened, I jolted my parents awake to tell them I had stolen a million dollars and was in *big* trouble. The premise of the night terror was always ridiculous. But the fear wasn't. The fear was all too real—the kind that crawls into the marrow of your bones and infects you. The kind of fear you feel when you're completely exposed, all your defenses are gone, and there's nothing left standing between you and the darkness.

What do you do when you need a shield to face the terrors of your night? To whom—or what—do you turn for protection?

Saint Paul says the true darkness we face in this world is not the forces of flesh and blood but rather the flaming arrows of the evil one. He says this darkness is so expansive and these arrows so sharp that we cannot possibly face them alone. If we are to stand against evil, he says, we must clothe ourselves in the full armor of God.

Years ago, a large and influential group of Christians boycotted Disney. They felt Disney's values no longer squared with theirs. I found this deeply troubling, mostly because I was in love with Ariel from *The Little Mermaid*. I share the story of this boycott because the image of faith as shield is a tricky one. If we conceive of faith primarily as a protective barrier keeping us from what we don't like or aren't comfortable with, then we miss the point. Paul doesn't say faith is a cocoon to wrap ourselves in but rather a shield to ward off attack.

Of course, you only need a shield if you're heading somewhere dangerous. And that is exactly where Christians are called to go. We run into the mess, not away from it. That's what Jesus does. Our Lord never runs from pain or sadness or illness or trouble. He walks straight into it, his arms wide open. When the religious leaders encircle a woman caught in adultery and want to stone her (which they have every legal right to do), Jesus dares those with no sin to throw the first stone. When a woman who has been bleeding for years (which Jewish society deemed unclean) touches Jesus, he allows his power to flow out of him and into her so she is healed on the spot. Jesus Christ willingly enters into controversial situations because he is far more concerned with the needs of others than he is with his own reputation.

My brothers and sisters, our faith calls us into the fray and toward the trouble. Not all of us are called to battle on the front lines, in dangerous mission fields near or far. We don't have to go to Calcutta,

India, like Mother Teresa. After all, we need only heed her advice: "Caluccttas are everywhere if only we have eyes to see. Find your Calcutta."

Somebody needs you. And your Christian duty is to go to this person. He or she may not be in an easy place—physically, emotionally, spiritually. Paul says flaming arrows will be involved—and they will be hurled right at you. A good priest once told me, "Be careful if you become friends with God. It's not the safest of relationships." Saint Paul knows that. That's why he uses battle imagery to describe the spiritual life. Following Jesus isn't easy; it never has been.

This brings us back to the shield. If we don't have a shield of faith to protect us, we won't last long, because life, while beautiful and magical, is also brutal and unfair and hard. So what is this shield? What does it look like?

Rick Warren, author of *The Purpose Driven Life*, preached a sermon shortly after his son's suicide. Warren preached that he had prayed every day for twenty-seven years for God to heal his son's mental illness. This was the number one prayer of his life, and it was never answered. As the service closed, Warren lifted a Bible above his head and said, "You give and you take away; my heart will choose to say, 'Lord, blessed be your name.'"

There is no way to explain that kind of strength apart from God. This is a man who doesn't merely have faith in God but a man who trusts in the faithfulness of God.

You see the difference? It's not just about mustering up belief but trusting that God is who he says he is: a good and faithful Father who will never leave us.

The shield of faith is God. Proverbs 30:5 says: "Every word of God proves true; he is a shield for those who take refuge in him."

God calls us to join the fray, but the good news is that God is already there. We never go alone or unprotected. We never stand fully exposed because we have a shield whose power is wider and stronger than any force in heaven or on earth or under the earth.

That doesn't mean bad things won't happen. They will. But we have a refuge.

So the question becomes whether or not we'll take comfort in God's refuge. Will we find our Calcutta and let the shield of faith cover us?

I got hit with a flaming arrow once. It was the arrow of doubt, and it hurt badly.

I doubted prayer. I just wasn't sure it made any difference. So I stopped praying. If it didn't make a difference, then it wouldn't matter whether I prayed or not. I carried on like this for nearly a year. The only way I can describe how I felt during that year is to ask you to imagine being without food or water for months and somehow staying alive. I was completely empty.

When I finally opened my heart again to prayer, I experienced resurrection. Our God is faithful—so very faithful—even when we are not.

I don't know what arrows are being shot at you, but I know they are coming hot and heavy. I also know some of you have already been hit. You need a shield. The good news is that you already have one. All you have to do is pick it up.

When I was having night terrors, there was only one way to calm me down. My father would guide me back to my room, help me into bed, and lie down beside me. I was thirteen years old, but I needed my father. He would put his arm around me and whisper, "It's okay, son, I'm here. I'm here. You can sleep now."

It's good to have the protection we need, isn't it?

The arrows will fly, and some will hit us. But the wounds, no matter how deep, are not fatal. Battles may rage, but the war has already been won.

Take refuge in the Lord and remember that God takes care of even the lilies and sparrows. God will take care of you. May you, in your day of trouble, stand and say: "You give and you take away, but my heart will choose to say, 'Lord, blessed be your name!'"

friends
or
servants?

You are my friends if you do what I command you. I do not call you servants any longer, because the servant does not know what the master is doing; but I have called you friends, because I have made known to you everything that I have heard from my Father. You did not choose me but I chose you. And I appointed you to go and bear fruit, fruit that will last, so that the Father will give you whatever you ask him in my name. I am giving you these commands so that you may love one another.

John 15:14-17

If you are anything like me, then you're really good at repeating mistakes. You say the thing you promised you wouldn't, and then you say it again. You spend the money you know you shouldn't, but then you make a little more money, and you go ahead and spend that too.

We repeat our mistakes. This is part of being human. We can know what is right and *still* fail to do it. Saint Paul describes it this way. "I do not understand my own actions. For I do not do what I want, but I do the very thing I hate" (Romans 7:15).

Ever felt that way?

After college I worked at a store called Luke's Locker selling running shoes. This basically amounted to me crouching on my knees and touching other people's feet all day long. I don't like feet. Feet are gross, and runners' feet are really gross. I can say this because I'm a runner, and my feet are all kinds of weird.

Some of my customers were kind to me—others, not so much. A certain dynamic comes into play when a person falls to his knees and handles someone's feet. If you've ever cleaned a toilet, bussed a table, or valeted a car, chances are you know what I'm talking about: being treated as *less than* because of the job you're working, or the car you're driving, or the house you're living in. We do this to each other. We label and we separate and we judge. And some of us get placed up high by those metrics, and some of us get placed down low.

Some of us are considered masters in this world, and others of us are servants.

There is a better way.

Read Jesus' words again: "I do not call you servants any longer, because the servant does not know what the master is doing; but I have called you friends, because I have made known to you everything that I have heard from my Father."

I have called you friends.

When you stop and think about it, this is a strange thing for Jesus to say. He is the Son of God, our Lord and Savior. How can *we* be his friends? Who among us is worthy of that title? I'm certainly not.

A popular t-shirt a few years back had a drawing of Christ and emblazoned with the words JESUS IS MY HOMEBOY. I never knew what to make of that shirt. Was it derogatory? A light-hearted joke? Cool? I never figured it out, although I admit that I wanted one. I still want that shirt. But calling Jesus my homeboy seems odd because I *worship* Jesus. I get down on my knees and beg Jesus to empower me and to forgive my sins. I don't do that with my homeboys.

But Jesus calls me his friend. Me. And you.

The great preacher Fred Craddock said, "If you have been all your life a servant of Jesus; if you've chosen that role…then to be called by Jesus his friend is an overwhelming gift."

What a marvelous and undeserved gift…

Consider the nature of friendship for a moment. Friendship is a bond between two people. No agenda, no ulterior motive. True friends aren't friends because they get something from each other; they're friends because they *care about* each other. That's what's so wonderful about genuine friendship. You look across the table and know the person sitting with you is there because they want to be. Is there anything else that feels so good?

Jesus loves us for who we are, not for what we can give. We are his friends, not his servants. What an incredible gift! But friendship, true friendship, though free, also costs something. Because we love one another, we listen to one another. And listening has consequences. When I listen, I come to know. And when I know, I must go and do.

I was eating lunch at a restaurant with a friend the other day when he asked me how I was doing. I wasn't doing well. I told him so. I was stressed, rundown, and worried about my health. I told him all of this with great emotion.

He said, "I'm sorry." Then he looked at the menu. "Do you want guacamole? Because I want guacamole." Then he ordered guacamole.

What. The. Heck?

Good friends listen, and then they do something about what they've just heard. They don't simply order guacamole. Friendship carries a cost. Listening has consequences.

So what do we hear as Jesus' friends. Read his words again. "I do not call you servants any longer, because the servant does not know what the master is doing; but I have called you friends, because I have made known to you everything that I have heard from my Father."

Put simply: We know what the Master knows.

I was at the doctor's office; the lab tech drawing my blood looked at my briefcase and said, "Carry your work around in that thing?"

"Yeah," I said.

"Does your work follow you everywhere you go?" he asked.

"Yeah, I guess it does."

"Not me," he said. "I love my work, but I don't take it home."

"Thanks for the judgment," I said. "And the needle in my arm."

He didn't know what to do with my response.

Look, I'm happy for that lab guy, but the truth is, the only reason he goes home carefree is because somebody else doesn't. I promise you the doctor who owns the practice loses sleep over the clinic. Masters carry burdens that others don't. And there is no master who carries more than *the* Master.

Have you ever considered the burden Jesus carries? The Master knows things I don't want to know. The Master knows that in the United States last year, more than 14,000 people were murdered.

The Master knows the number of hairs on the head of each of the victims. He knows their names—knew them before they were ever born. The Master also knows that a hundred students who attend the high school across the street from my church are homeless. The Master feels the pain of each and every one of them. The Master knows all sorts of things I don't want to know.

But maybe I need to know these things, these people? Maybe *knowing* is the only path to *loving*.

After all, this is our command. "Love one another," Jesus says, "as I have loved you...you are my friends if you do what I command you."

Friendship carries a cost.

Theologian Douglas Hare said that "in an age when the word 'love' is greatly abused, we must remember the primary component of biblical love is not affection, but commitment...to love our neighbor does not mean to feel affection for them, but to imitate God in taking their needs seriously."[1]

If we are to follow and imitate Christ, we cannot view one another as servants but as friends—friends who need each other. When we forget this, we treat each other poorly.

Rarely do we make a mistake that we never make again. However in high school I made a mistake that I have managed to avoid repeating. *Thank God.*

I was eating at Chili's with my friends, which is what we did every weekend because we had wildly sophisticated palates. It was either Chili's or TGI Fridays. That's it. I'm not even sure we were aware other restaurants existed. Anyway, we were there, it

---

1 (Brian Stoffregen quoting Douglas Hare, Interpretation Commentaries, p. 260).

was crowded, and our waitress wasn't (in my insanely immature opinion) cutting it. I wanted my Coke refilled, and I couldn't get her attention. For my sixteen-year-old brain, this constituted a major crisis. So, as she walked by our table, I reached out my hand toward her and snapped my fingers. "Excuse me," I said.

I know. I know. I know.

Take a moment to mourn whatever perception you had of me up until this point. Yes, I snapped my fingers at another human being as if she were my property. Try not to hate me too, too much. I still feel really badly about this.

The waitress heard the snap, stopped walking, and came toward me. She bent down at our table until our faces were *very* close to one another. She was gorgeous, a fact I hadn't noticed until that moment. And she smelled like lavender. All of this served to intensify my sudden panic. She said, "Did you just snap your fingers at me?"

I nodded and the table went silent.

"Are you in high school?" she asked.

I gulped. "Yes, ma'am."

"I'm going to give you some advice," she said. "*Never* do that again. It's not right." She stood upright and smoothed out her apron. "Now…what was it that you so desperately needed?"

I felt about one inch tall. "A coke," I whispered ashamedly.

"One Coke. Coming right up." She smiled warmly and walked away.

It's easy to treat people badly, isn't it? When people offer us a service, it's easy to see them as the service and not as people, as a means to an end instead of living, breathing human beings. This is wrong. It's sinful. And yet I do it all the time. I grow impatient with my waiter who should just write down my order instead of incorrectly memorizing it. My doctor doesn't return my phone call fast enough. The car in front of me needs to exit the left lane so I can make my meeting on time. When we commoditize other people primarily in terms of what they can or cannot do for us, we drift from Jesus' vision of us treating one another as friends, and not as servants.

Think of it like this. If you know a coworker is struggling because his mother is battling Alzheimer's, then it's more difficult to be cruel when he drops the ball and makes you look bad in front of your boss. It's nearly impossible to ignore a person's pain when you know her spouse has filed for divorce. It's tough to snap your fingers at a waitress when you know she's a single mom trying to raise two kids. People aren't just people—they're *people*—and they all have stuff going on.

The Master cares deeply about *all* that stuff, the stuff you and I sometimes don't want to know. But the Master says we need to know because we need to love.

But let's not kid ourselves. This is not easy.

The other morning I was in Dunkin' Donuts getting coffee. The woman in front of me was giving the cashier a hard time. "I normally go through the drive-thru," she said. "But the last three times, my order has been wrong."

The cashier apologized.

"Now, I don't know who is working today, but you just need to know my order has been wrong, and I want it to be right this time."

"Yes, ma'am," the cashier said. "Of course. What can I get you?"

"The last three times y'all have put sugar in my coffee. I don't want sugar put in my coffee."

"I understand," the cashier said. "I'll make sure your order this morning is correct. No sugar."

"I want a medium hazelnut coffee with one cream." She paused. "No sugar."

"Oh," the cashier said with a grin. "I see what the issue might have been. We have two kinds of hazelnut coffee. One is sugar-free and the other has an artificial sweetener in it. Which one have you been ordering?"

The woman huffed. Seriously. She literally huffed. "I didn't know there was a choice. Nobody told me there was a choice."

"There's our problem." The cashier smiled again. He then punched in the order. "Let's get you a sugar-free, medium hazelnut coffee. I think that's what you want."

"I have another question," the woman said. "At other Dunkin' Donuts, they have large travel mugs you can buy and get free refills."

There were now three people behind me waiting in line. It was past 8 a.m., and we all had some places to be.

"Do y'all have those mugs for purchase?"

The cashier politely finished making her coffee before showing her the refillable mugs. The rest of us waited while she perused the mugs ,eventually deciding she didn't really want one. Then she stormed out of the shop, seemingly more angry than when she came in.

As I drove away, I couldn't help but think of some headlines from the week's news.

Terrorists bombed a Christian picnic on Sunday morning, killing nearly a hundred women and children. A woman in a nearby city was charged with the murder of her two children. When the police arrested her, she asked, "Did I do something bad?" A couple of days later, a mother was murdered while setting up an early morning fitness class in a church parking lot.

I have been that person getting mad about my coffee. I've honked at the person in front of me at the red light. I've intentionally sped up to keep that annoying truck from moving into my lane. I've been a jerk. Ask anyone who has ever known me. I've withheld apologies, sent snippy text messages, laid out one last argument instead of walking away in peace. I've been petty. I've been small. And all of these have been wasted moments. I may not be able to thwart the plans of terrorists or keep sick people from harming children, but I *can* be kind. I can treat those I encounter in all situations, even the most mundane, as sacred creations of God. And in doing so, perhaps I can offer life and love and light into this world that may someday circle all the way back around to bless some person on the verge of committing some heinous act. Who knows?

I can't control everything or fix everything. But I can change my behavior. I know that love is a better way, and so love must be our way. We are all in this together. We just are, and the sooner we accept this, the better it's going to be.

We don't have all the answers at this moment. The world is grossly complex. But there is one thing we can all do in whatever city or circumstances we find ourselves. It's so simple: We can be genuinely kind.

I wonder what tomorrow might look like if we all gave kindness an honest try. Every encounter is a chance to treat someone as either servant or a friend. When Jesus encountered us, he chose friend. What a gift. All he asks in return is that we give it to someone else.

dragon tracks*

He has removed our sins as far from us as the east is from the west.—New Living Translation

Psalm 103:12

*[Urban Dictionary: n. said of an object that may have had a shady history, or was possibly used in a crime in a previous owner's hands]

When I taught high school, I led daily noonday prayer services. Afterward, I would take the long way from the chapel to the cafeteria where I was responsible for maintaining the peace between ravenous savages...I mean...delightful adolescent angels.

Have you had the pleasure of dining in a high school cafeteria lately? It's what I imagine prison might be like, only scarier. Here's some advice. If you find yourself in the path of a 17-year-old boy in need of a chicken sandwich—run. Fast. He *will* eat you if it comes down to it.

We did have some real angels on our campus though. Just outside the chapel, elementary students played during recess. Each day as I would pass them, a few of the children would smile, and I would smile and wave back. For this moment, all was right in the world. I looked forward to this exchange every day: It revived my soul to see innocent children at play.

One afternoon one of the little girls surprised me. "Excuse me," she said. "We were wondering something about you."

"What's that?" I asked.

She got a little nervous, looked back over her shoulder at her friends who were watching from a safe distance. "Well…" she began slowly, "We want to know whether you're a man or…just a *tall* boy?"

Have these kids been talking to my wife?

I said, "Well, what do *you* think?"

"We *think* you're a man."

I laughed. "I *think* you're right."

She smiled and pointed to one of the little boys standing in the background. "Now," she said, "he's a boy, a very bad boy. He does everything the teacher says not to."

I looked over at the little boy and recognized a naughty look in his eyes. It was the same one I've seen in the mirror my whole life.

I said to him, "You don't look so bad."

He eyeballed me as only a six-year-old can, jutted out his chin, and said, "No. It's true. I'm a very bad boy." Then he ran off.

I walked to the cafeteria, turning his words over in my mind. *I'm a very bad boy.* On one level he was joking, right? He knew this answer would get a rise out of me. But on another level, he wasn't joking. He was naughty, and he wasn't afraid to say it out loud. Children are often surprisingly good at being honest about who and how they are. We adults are a little different. We like to gloss over things and pretend they're not nearly as bad as they are. We all do this, and we know it's madness: We can either confront problems or allow them to metastasize into full-blown crises.

Jesus is chatting with some priests, and he tells them a story from Matthew. *A man has two sons, and he says to the first, 'Go and work in the vineyard today.'*

No thanks, the son answers. *I've got other plans.* But then he changes his mind and does as his father asks. The father goes to the second son, giving the same command. *Yes sir!* he says. But then he changes his mind and does *not* do as his father has asked. Which son does the will of his father?

Easy, the priests say. *The one who goes and actually works the vineyard.*

Correct, Jesus says.

Now the text doesn't say this but I imagine that Jesus pauses and waits for them to get it—to understand that in condemning the second son, they condemn themselves. But they don't. So Jesus says, *You know those tax collectors you despise and prostitutes you judge? They will arrive at heaven's door long before you ever will.*

Excuse me, Jesus! Those people are sinners!

That's right, Jesus says. *Just like you. The difference is, they are willing to admit it.*

Now that hits close to home for me. I have sin in my life. I have done things in my past that I'm ashamed of, things for which I still feel guilt. I know God has forgiven me, but these moments still turn my stomach just the same. Sometimes I'll be preaching and think,

What if all these people knew the things I've done and said? What if they read my text messages or saw my Internet search history? Would they still listen to me? Would they even talk to me?

The ever-present danger of the religious life is beginning to believe we are better than we actually are. Morally bankrupt people don't believe that, which is why they're sometimes better at repenting. They're honest and often willing to say, "I've been a bad boy. My past is shady. There are dragon tracks all over me."

We religious folk don't want to admit this. But we *need* to because it's true. Once we acknowledge our sinful behavior, come clean about where we have failed, we arrive at a place of scandalous honesty—and that's where we find grace.

I'll be honest; repentance isn't my favorite religious word. I like words like "blessing" and "love" and "mercy." Repentance? I'll pass, if that's all right. The catch is that repentance is the only thing John the Baptist ever preaches. And it is the *first* thing Jesus preaches. Have you ever thought about that? John the Baptist was the man sent to "prepare the way of the Lord" (Mark 1:3). How does he do it? By asking people to repent for the forgiveness of their sins. Then, when Jesus shows up on the scene and preaches his first sermon, it's pretty clear he's been listening to John because he simply repeats what John has been saying all along. These are the words of Jesus' first sermon as recorded in Mark: "The time is fulfilled, and the kingdom of God has come near; repent, and believe in the good news."

Repent, Jesus says. *Repent.*

But…still? Who wants to do this? "Repent" evokes such negative feelings of guilt and shame. But what if it didn't have to? Strictly speaking, repent means to make a change. That's it. That's all the word repent actually means.

Jesus says, "I am the way, truth, and the life" (John 14:6). In other words, would you like to come *my* way? Would you like to *repent*?

Would it be all right if I asked you a question? No one else is listening—it's just you and me.

Do you believe God loves you? When you hear the Bible say that God desires the death of no person but wants to give us life—do you buy it?

I hope you do because life is what repentance is all about. *Life*. It's about turning away from death and choosing life. Wherever you are, whatever habit has a hold on your life, its grip is not stronger than the love of Christ. And your actions, no matter how secret or shameful, cannot separate you from that love.

I've heard it said that God loves the sinner just as much as the saint. The only difference is that the saint knows she is loved. Think about Peter and Judas. Both men betray Jesus. But Peter knows he is loved and can go back. Judas doesn't know this. Or, if he does, he doesn't truly believe it.

It's hard to go back to God after wandering and sinning. There's a reason Adam and Eve hid from God after they had eaten the forbidden fruit—none of us like being faced with our sins. We don't want to look at what we've done, and we definitely don't want anyone else looking at it—especially God! It's scary to be really seen for what we are in our unsavory, shady places. This is why we pretend we don't have dragon tracks on our lives. But the truth is that it's only through embracing our dragon tracks that we can be freed from them. Problems are either dealt with or left to metastasize.

Christians talk a lot about truth, but we're mostly afraid of it. We like to quote Saint John and say the truth sets us free, but most of us are too scared to get anywhere near the truth.

Honestly, there are very few instances where we actually tell the truth. Most folks walk through life putting up fronts, exaggerating, and avoiding. There just aren't many places you can find where people are truly committed to honesty. The church is supposed to be one of those places.

Before I met my wife, I dated a lovely young woman I had known since college. We dated seriously for about two years. We talked about marriage. I loved her, and she loved me. But I had some trouble during those days. I was deeply unhappy with my career choice, and, if I'm being totally honest, I drank too much. That's a hard sentence to write. But it's true. I got drunk fairly often and sometimes couldn't remember what I had said or done the night before. If you've ever done that, you know how bad this feels. These are my dragon tracks. Even as I write these words, I want to pretend they're not mine. I want to pretend my past isn't shady, to pretend I've never done anything wrong. But I am not going to do that. I am not going to do that.

So, I reached a breaking point, and I decided I needed to make some changes in my life because for the first time I didn't really like who I was. I had no idea what these changes needed to be, but for some reason I thought they involved breaking up with this kind and patient woman. So that's what I did. I blindsided my best friend and told her I didn't want to marry her.

And I left. I refused to be honest about my pain and I also refused to listen to hers. I just cut ties and ran. If we had been teenagers, this might have been okay. But we were full-grown adults. What I did was cruel and selfish.

We didn't see or speak to one another for seven years.

Then she walked into a coffee shop where I was sipping a cappuccino. We locked eyes and had one moment to decide what we were going to do. You know that moment of sheer terror. We moved toward one another; she went for the hug while I stuck out my hand for the shake. Awkward. I pulled my hand in as fast as humanly possible, and we shared a hug that could have gone viral had it been recorded, such was the level of discomfort between us.

You can imagine the first few minutes of our exchange. Standard, stilted talk about what we were each up to. She had become a successful television and film producer, and I was married with two kids. The conversation probably lasted two minutes, but it felt like forever. Nervously, I told her I didn't want to make her late for work and said goodbye. As I walked away, I heard the voice of God in my heart.

Apologize, God said. *Tell her you're sorry. Repent. Do it now.*

A wave of fear rushed over my body, and my heart rate soared. I didn't want to apologize. I wanted to sprint out the door. But in a moment of rare obedience, I stood back up and walked over to her and said without qualification, "I'm sorry." A long silence ensued. "I'm so sorry for hurting you." I took a breath. "I never told you that. I'm terribly, terribly sorry."

I had no idea what was about to happen. I probably deserved a slap across the face, but she didn't do that. She smiled warmly and said, "Ryan, it's all right. It was all so long ago."

"No, but I'm sorry. I should have told you what I was going through. I should have opened up and been honest with you. What I did wasn't right."

"Thank you," she said.

"Do you have a minute to talk?" I asked.

She did. We sat down, and for half an hour, we were really honest with one another. Brimming with grace, she sat and listened to me apoligize for the damage I had caused. I can't imagine this was easy for her. There were moments I was certain she would start crying. But she just kept listening and exuding empathy, mercy, and love.

God is like this woman. It doesn't matter how many years go by or how much sin we commit. When we make a turn, when we repent, God is waiting with an open heart to forgive.

God will sit in that coffee shop with us. God is big enough for our truth. God is big enough for our mistakes. God is big enough for the total disasters we make of our lives, and God wants to hear all of it. God wants to hear about it so he can tell us we don't have to choose death—we can choose the way of life.

One afternoon after chapel, I walked past the children outside the chapel when the "bad little boy" ran up to me and said, "Guess what?! Guess what?!"

"What?"

"Today, I was a *really* good boy."

"Yes," I said. "I believe that."

to
kill a
brother

Cain said to his brother Abel, "Let us go out to the field." And when they were in the field, Cain rose up against his brother Abel, and killed him.

Genesis 4:8

Dear God,

It's me, Ryan Casey.

I'm kind of dying down here today.

As I write this, two men have been shot and killed by police within the past two days. Two black men. One was on the ground, straddled by the police when they shot him. The other man had been pulled over for a broken taillight. The arresting officer shot the man multiple times while he was reaching for his license and registration. His girlfriend live streamed his final moments on Facebook.

I don't even know what to say.

I've always respected police officers. When I was a child, I asked for their autographs. They were real-life superheroes! They still are. Growing up, I dreamed of becoming a police officer. I couldn't imagine anything more noble than donning a uniform and running toward danger to help people. But then I grew older and became selfish and fearful of such a high calling. The men and women who wear blue are some of our absolute finest citizens. One of the cops who patrols our neighborhood always flashes his lights for my three-year-old son. It's such a kind gesture. There are so many brave and good police officers, so many.

But these other guys, they have got to stop shooting black people. They just have to.

God, please stop the violence. Please stamp out our racism. Help us see one another as the precious works of creation we are. Please remind us that we are nothing less than brothers and sisters. We are blood of each other's blood. Help us stop shedding it.

Why is it so natural for us to hurt and kill one another? I guess that's why you told us about Cain and Abel at the very beginning of the Bible. I mean, we don't make it through the fourth chapter of the first book before we witness the first murder. It spins my head.

Three years ago, I watched my wife pull out of a parking lot with our son in the backseat. She cut off another driver—it was an accident. The other driver slammed on the brakes and narrowly avoided rear-ending her. My mother-in-law was also in the car.

I breathed a sigh of relief and then began backing my own car out of the parking lot, thinking a disaster had been averted. But then I saw something in my rear view mirror that told me it wasn't over. The woman in the other car had jumped out and was running toward my wife's car. I threw my car back into park, jumped out, and started running too.

By the time I got to the car, the woman was cursing and banging her fists against my wife's window. She was also trying to open the door to the backseat where our infant child was. I managed to wedge my body between her and the car and asked her to back up. She refused. She was a hard-looking woman. Her t-shirt was cut so short that it barely covered her breasts. She wasn't wearing shoes. But that isn't what made her seem hard—it was her eyes. They were as angry as any I had ever seen. A chill ran down my spine.

"Please just back up." I asked. She refused. I apologized for my wife. "It was just an accident," I said. "She didn't mean to cut you off." I motioned to my wife to keep her window rolled up.

The woman wasn't interested in what I had to say. She made another push for the car, and I had to put my hands on her to keep her from opening a door. My wife began to pull away. It was a bizarre moment. Less than ten minutes earlier, I had been popping a piece of sushi in my mouth. Now I was standing in the middle of a busy street in a physical struggle with a woman who looked like she could beat the crap out of me.

I don't really remember what happened between my wife pulling away and the woman and I walking back to her car. But somehow we began moving in that direction. Her car was idling in the street, the door wide open. Traffic was starting to back up.

We were almost back to her car when she stopped and turned to face me. "You're wife's crazy!" she said. "Driving like that with a baby in the car? What a bitch."

"It was an accident," I said. "She's sorry. I'm sorry. Why don't you just get back in your—" *Pop!* A right hook caught me completely unaware. Her fist caught my Adam's apple on its way to my jaw. I reflectively clutched my throat and staggered backward.

"That's what you get!" She threw a few other choice words at me before jumping in her car and speeding away. She blew right through a red light and out of my sight.

I spent nearly every afternoon of my childhood and adolescence in martial arts—I've been punched before. But this was the hardest anyone had ever hit me. I found myself standing in the street, gasping for air, wondering: *What just happened?*

Over the next few days, I spent a surprising number of hours fantasizing about punching that woman back. It's shameful to admit but true. I wondered what it would feel like to retaliate. Her violence was so unnecessary and the things she said were so vile. I wanted to punch her. I truly did.

But I didn't, and I know I never would. But if I'm being candid, I must admit that this thought stayed with me for weeks. Weeks. One night, I dreamed I was pummeling her face with my bloodied knuckles. I woke up in a panicked sweat, sick to my stomach.

I want so badly to be a pacifist, but the truth is I feel an electric hum of violence in me. When I'm physically assaulted, my immediate reaction is not to retreat. My nature is to hit you back harder than you hit me. When I was a younger man, I shamefully admit I did just that.

But violence is awful. If you've ever been on the receiving end, you know this is true. And if you have ever doled it out, you know being violent does not come without a cost. Our fists have memories all their own.

I am disgusted by what's happening in our world—mass shootings, road rage, terrorist attacks. I watch the news and feel a deep part of me yearn for a violent solution. There's part of me that wants our military to start bombing terrorists and our police to patrol the streets with a liberal use of force…Maybe that is the way to end this chaos.

And yet I can't help but remember the words of Martin Luther King Jr., who responded to violence and vitriol not with an equal measure of force, but with love. "Hate cannot drive out hate, and darkness cannot drive out darkness," he said. "Only love and light can do those things."

I don't know the proper way forward through these distressing times. I honestly don't. But I do know that if light and love aren't playing a central role in our strategy, we will be stuck in this loop of violence forever. That can't be God's plan. There must be a better way.

I worked with a man who lived in China for nearly a decade. He met a Chinese woman who later became his wife. I asked him about his wife's view of Christianity because she is Buddhist and he is Catholic, and I am nosy.

My friend said, "Oh, she loves Christianity. Adores the music, the liturgy, the grand stories of the Bible. She especially likes the teachings of Jesus."

"Well, that's good," I said.

He held up a finger. "But there's one thing she can't get past, one thing she doesn't understand."

"What?"

"*That.*" He pointed to the cross around my neck. "For the life of her, she can't understand why Christians put suffering at the center of faith."

Not a bad question.

In case you don't know, many Buddhists believe that the first thing one must understand about life is that it is full of suffering. I heard a man at a funeral say that by age six, children understand death. By age ten, they understand that death applies to them. It doesn't take long for children to become acquainted with suffering. But the great hope taught by Buddha is that suffering can be overcome. From this viewpoint, suffering is a hurdle that must be jumped and left behind. But Christianity allows suffering to take center stage—and we leave it right there through the curtain call.

Why do we do this? Different Christians offer different explanations, but here's one I find compelling: Christians focus on a crucified Christ because the crucifixion happened. Jesus didn't "regard equality with God as something to be exploited but emptied himself, taking the form of a slave, and was obedient to the point of death—even death on a cross" (Philippians 2:6).

On Palm Sunday, the bulk of the Jewish community in Jerusalem are expecting Jesus to conquer the Romans and vanquish their suffering. But Jesus arrives and says, *I'm not gonna do that. I won't answer violence with violence. But I will do something. I will go down to the valley, where the shadows are longest, and I will die right beside you.*

I read about a Dutch priest who lived in Syria for nearly fifty years. Before he was murdered, a reporter asked him why he hadn't left with other Westerners when the rebels took over. His answer: "The Syrian people have given me so much—so much kindness, inspiration, everything. If they're suffering now, I want to share their pain."

I want to share their pain.

Wow. The Buddhists may be on to something: Life is suffering, which means only a suffering God can help.

This is why Jesus doesn't violently oust the Romans. He could call upon legions of angels and wage a holy war. But he chooses not to. He doesn't kill his enemies, and he won't kill ours. Jesus has not promised to fight our enemies or remove our troubles. Instead he offers something very different.

> *I'll lie down in that cancer bed with you. Your suffering will be my suffering.*
>
> *I'll stand beside you while you bury the love of your life.*
>
> *I'll hold your hand when you're gripped so tight with anxiety you can scarcely breathe.*
>
> *I'll raise you up every time you fall. I promise.*
>
> *I'll be your friend when you don't have one.*

Our God is a suffering God. This is not a morbid theology—it's wildly good news. This perspective helps me a lot when I want to ball up my fists and punch back because it reminds me that violence does nothing but beget violence.

I think the woman who punched me was deeply suffering. I don't think she was actually angry with my wife or with me. I think she was overwhelmed and needed some place to put her fist for a moment in time. So she put it on me. That doesn't make what she did right but it does make it easier to pray for her. That is precisely what Jesus has done for those who betrayed, beat, and killed him.

With this kind of forgiveness in mind, maybe today we can all pray for each other. Maybe we can pray for those who suffer, for victims of violence, and for those who commit violence. Maybe we can then celebrate those who prize peace, love, and the dignity of all human life. Maybe we can slow down our judgement of those who insist on violence. And then maybe we can stand together and declare that even though we've been shedding one another's blood from the beginning of time, the cycle can be stopped.

Maybe the stopping can start with us.

don't
touch
the heart

"Be perfect, therefore, as your heavenly Father
is perfect."

Matthew 5:48

I stood in the darkened gymnasium, waiting for it to happen. Creased khakis, Tommy Hilfiger necktie, and hard-earned coiffed hair, I felt as suave as a 13-year-old James Bond. The occasion was Valentine's Day, but the moment was destiny.

The week before, every student in our school filled out a love questionnaire, which was then entered into a mysterious computer program that promised to match each student with his or her soul mate. The pairings were to be announced at the dance.

I could not have been more excited. I already knew my soul mate: Lauren. She had righteously blonde hair and an amazing smile. Plus, I had caught her looking at me in class—more than once. She was perfect.

On this night, my heart would reveal this love. I knew that my name and hers would be matched, and we would live happily ever after in middle-school-wedded bliss.

But something unexpected happened. A teacher took the stage and said there would be one announcement before the couples were revealed. It turned out that only two names were a perfect match.

A furtive murmur filled the gym, as kids wondered who the lucky couple could be. But I didn't wonder. I straightened my tie because I knew my name was about to be called. And a second later it was. As I made my way to the stage to receive my bride, the other shoe dropped. "And Ryan's perfect match," the teacher said, "is none other than our very own principal…Mrs. Laurie Fetter!"

I don't remember much about the ensuing chaos. I'm pretty sure I had an out-of-body experience. When I came to, I was hiding in the boy's locker room, determined to stay there for all of time and eternity in the fetal position.

It wasn't just the humiliation of being matched with the principal. That was bad. Really bad. But I was crushed because this was supposed to be the night when the secrets of my heart escaped from my chest, when I could declare with scientific certainty that Lauren was my match.

Alas, this was not to be.

Ever felt that way? Have you ever had a burning deep within you that you longed to express? Have you felt your heart leading you toward something or someone? Or, have you felt the opposite: a darker desire that you would do anything to keep secret?

It's tough to deny the heart, isn't it? Long ago, Christian theologian and mathematician Blaise Pascal said, "The heart has its reasons of which reason knows nothing."

In the Bible, the heart is the seat of both the emotions and the intellect; it is the core of the person, the true, real self. Your heart is the self known only to you and God, your most intimate self.

That is why the verse from Matthew is so terribly uncomfortable. We know our hearts, and we know they are anything but perfect. These kinds of verses always make me think of Thomas Jefferson's personal Bible, which was made public only after his death. He took a razor and cut out all the parts that he didn't like. Jefferson thought Jesus was a great moral teacher but didn't care for the so-called miracle stories. So he snipped them out. Feeding the poor? Clothing the naked? Jefferson decided all that could stay. But walking on water? Healing the blind? Jefferson thought all of this was the stuff of children's bedtime stories, not serious historical narrative.

It's tempting to adopt Jefferson's strategy for reading the Bible—just ignore the uncomfortable bits. The problem is that we can't. Jefferson was undoubtedly brilliant, but it's foolish to skip the uncomfortable parts. Because these parts touch our hearts.

> *You've heard it said, Don't murder, but I say anger and name-calling are enough to send you to hell.*
>
> *You've heard it said, Don't commit adultery, but I say lust in the heart is just as dangerous.*
>
> *I know Moses said you could divorce your wife, but unless there's sexual betrayal, you had better not.*
>
> *I'm aware swearing in court is customary, but I say be so filled with integrity that people trust your word. Don't even bother taking a vow.*
>
> *And don't even think about coming to the altar to ask for my forgiveness until you've done so with your brothers and sisters. Want reconciliation with your God in heaven? Seek it first with the people you've wronged.*

If you're ratcheting up to a panic attack, don't worry. I am too! Especially because Jesus is just getting started.

Jesus goes on to say that in the old days, it was an eye for an eye and a tooth for a tooth, but the time has come to turn the other cheek, to give to every person who begs, and to love all people—especially the ones who hate us. In fact, he says if our love doesn't extend to our enemies, then our love is—to put it crudely—cheap. And then, when we positively can take no more, Jesus kicks us while we're down, saying: "Be perfect as your heavenly Father is perfect."

Maybe Jefferson cut out the wrong parts. I say let's keep the water-to-wine business and toss these difficult parts out. But we can't. Because all of scripture is holy and God wants us to hear it. All of it.

But what does this command to be perfect mean? If Jesus dies for our sins and offers grace, why does Jesus inject the Ten Commandments with steroids by telling us to be perfect? Life is already hard enough.

Be perfect? Who can do that? This is giving me a complex.

Truckloads of theological ink have been spilled interpreting this passage. Some say Jesus is simply exposing how sinful we are in an effort to get us on our knees to beg forgiveness. Maybe.

Others say, no, Jesus is intensifying the law, not to expose our sinfulness but to literally call us to a higher level of righteousness, one he fully expects us to attain. Perhaps. The trouble is that this feels impossible.

Let's get real. Most of us won't struggle to keep from taking an ax and murdering our neighbor. Murder just isn't our thing. But calling a friend a fool? Guilty. Most will honor marital vows but controlling every passionate thought? Doubt it. It was this very passage that former President Jimmy Carter referenced when he said he had committed adultery in his heart. The press ate him alive, but he was just being honest, trying to take Jesus seriously.

While Carter said he hadn't cheated on his wife, he acknowledged that he fell far short of the standard of perfection Christ gives. Haven't we all?

At this point we may be feeling like the football players at the University of Texas when former Head Coach Charlie Strong issued his expectations of his players.[1] Below are the highlights.

> Players will attend all of their classes and sit in the first two rows. No headphones in class. No texting in class. Sit up and take notes.

> If a player misses class, he runs until it hurts. If he misses two classes, his entire position unit runs. If he misses three classes, his position coach runs. His position coach does not want to run.

> No drugs. No stealing. No guns. Treat women with respect. The team will live together, eat together, and suffer together.

> The focus will be winning and graduating; anything extraneous will be stamped out and removed.

Needless to say, a few players immediately transferred out of the University of Texas when these rules were published.

Rules. Just writing that word kind of irritates me. Who likes rules? Sure, these rules set out by the coach are good rules that will probably instill discipline and breed success. But…they're *just* rules, which means players will break them because that's what happens to rules. They break. They're good, and they're helpful, but they are just rules, and rules only have so much power.

---

1   http://www.barkingcarnival.com/2014/1/14/5308182/culture-change-at-texas

Rules can control a person, but rules will never change a person. Change has to come from within.

Jesus isn't talking rules—he's talking about transformation.

If the goal is to encourage our good behavior, Jesus could leave the law alone. The rules are clear. But compliance is not all Jesus wants. He wants our hearts. He doesn't want to control us; he wants to transform us.

The point isn't to keep from doing bad things. The point is to experience God's peace and purity in our hearts and minds. This passage isn't about Jesus micromanaging our hearts. It's just the opposite. Jesus wants to touch our hearts so we may live as God always intended. Perfectly.

And yet we still trip on that word. Perfect. Who, beyond Christ, is perfect? Who has full control of his or her thoughts? Who has tamed his or her heart? Not me. But this is what Matthew says to do.

So how are we to respond? Luke presents this same material as Matthew, and for the most part the message is similar. But at the end, Luke makes a change—and it's a real doozy. Where Matthew says, "Be perfect as your heavenly Father is perfect" Luke says "Be merciful, just as your Father is merciful." Isn't that lovely?

Daniel Clendinin, founder of the Journey with Jesus webzine, says, "No one can be perfect, but everyone can show mercy. And in showing mercy, we approach divine perfection."[2] I think he's absolutely right.

When the Pharisees challenge Jesus because he eats and drinks with sinners, Jesus says to them, "Go and learn what this means, 'I desire mercy, not sacrifice.' For I have come to call not the righteous but sinners" (Matthew 9:13).

Jesus Christ has come to earth so that the imperfect might know perfection through the flooding of our hearts with mercy. We will get angry with each other, but I'm curious how much heartache might be avoided if we nourished mercy in our hearts instead of revenge? Divorces will happen. Sometimes they *need* to happen. But do you ever wonder what our relationships could look like if we injected a dose of mercy into them? Sometimes we need vows, but what would life look like if we trusted one another a little more? How might our lives be enriched if we assumed the best, instead of the worst, in others?

Mercy does these things. The Bible says that while we were still sinners, Christ died for us. Before we ever did anything to deserve God's love, he gave it to us. All he asks is that we pay it forward.

What is in your heart today? Could your heart use a little mercy?

I eventually left the locker room and made my way back into the gym, where the Valentine's dance was underway. I wasn't about to let some computer program derail the desires of my heart. I walked straight up to Lauren and asked her to dance.

And we danced. It was magic.

Jesus understands that it is a truly human inclination to follow our hearts. He knows that whatever lurks in the shadows within will eventually make its way out into the light. Maybe not today. Maybe not tomorrow. But someday it will.

Human beings follow their hearts. So what's in the heart really, deeply matters. Do you know where I run into trouble with this whole concept? I will extend you mercy. This is not my problem.

My problem is that I won't offer it to myself. I'll forgive you, but I won't forgive myself. But that's not the gospel. I can't deny myself what God has already given me.

And neither can you.

So take a deep breath. Let it out.

Now do it again.

Then let God in.

To touch and perfect your heart with mercy and love.

this very night

Someone in the crowd said to him, "Teacher, tell my brother to divide the family inheritance with me." But he said to him, "Friend, who set me to be a judge or arbitrator over you?" And he said to them, "Take care! Be on your guard against all kinds of greed; for one's life does not consist in the abundance of possessions." Then he told them a parable: "The land of a rich man produced abundantly. And he thought to himself, 'What should I do, for I have no place to store my crops?' Then he said, 'I will do this: I will pull down my barns and build larger ones, and there I will store all my grain and my goods. And I will say to my soul, 'Soul, you have ample goods laid up for many years; relax, eat, drink, be merry.' But God said to him, 'You fool! This very night your life is being demanded of you. And the things you have prepared, whose will they be?' So it is with those who store up treasures for themselves but are not rich toward God."

Luke 12:13-21

A few months ago I read a haunting book, *When Breath Becomes Air.* It begins:

"I flipped through the CT scan images, the diagnosis obvious: the lungs were matted with innumerable tumors the spine deformed, a full lobe of the liver obliterated. Cancer, widely disseminated. I was a neurosurgical resident entering my final year of training. Over the last six years, I'd examined scores of such scans, on the off chance that some procedure might benefit the patient. But this scan was different: it was my own."

The author, Dr. Paul Kalanithi, died at age thirty-seven, almost two years after his diagnosis. He was nearly finished with his training when he became sick. He had an undergraduate degree from Stanford University, a medical degree from Yale School of Medicine, and a neurosurgery residency at Stanford. He was a year from settling into one of the most prestigious specialties in medicine and from enjoying the money and status that would come along with it. That's when he saw the scan—when he knew that in all likelihood, he was going to die.

Paul had to make some decisions. How would he spend his last days? What *is* worth doing when you can no longer pretend you'll live forever?

If you told me I would die in five minutes, I'd close my computer, find my wife and children, and hold them. That would be worth doing. Writing this book is worth doing, but there are a lot of authors and the world would probably be just fine without me. If I had five minutes, time with my family is what would matter most.

The great folk singer Bob Dylan says not to talk falsely now, for the hour is getting late.

It is. Whether we're young or old, healthy or sick, we are fleeting things—here one moment and gone the next. The reality is that we all have five minutes. We just pretend this isn't true until age or illness won't let us pretend anymore.

But compare that mindset with that of the psalmist:

"LORD let me know my end,
>   and what is the measure of my days;
>   let me know how fleeting my life is.

> You have made my days a few handbreadths,
>   and my lifetime is as nothing in your sight.
> Surely everyone stands as a mere breath."

Psalm 39:4-5

A mere breath. That is all we are—here one second and gone the next.

We have a small amount of time to decide what matters in life, even though most of us live as the rich man does in this chapter's parable, assuming we have many years ahead to sit back, relax, and enjoy the spoils of our accomplishments. But the truth is that we might not. "Fool!" God says to the rich man. "This very night your soul is required of you…"

Ever since I read Paul Kalanithi's book, I've wondered what he might say about this parable. Paul was a Christian so I assume he had read it. The parallel between his life and that of the rich man are obvious. They were two successful men who had gone to great lengths to secure their futures, only to be told they didn't have one.

You've saved, God says. *You've stored up treasure. What you haven't done is remember that you're merely a breath, here one moment and gone the next.*

When Paul was wrestling with what to do with his remaining days, he begged his oncologist for a timeline.

"I can't tell you that," she replied. "I can only say that you can get back to surgery if you want, but you have to figure out what's most important to you."

"If I had some sense of how much time I have left," Paul argued, "it'd be easier. If I had two years, I'd write. If I had ten, I'd get back to surgery…"

If we knew how much time we had, then we'd order our lives accordingly. *Right?*

Maybe. Two years? Ten years? Fifty? It's all just five minutes. Young or old, healthy or sick, the time is later than we think.

God says we are fools to think otherwise. Ouch. The word "fool" in the Bible is an especially harsh word. A fool, biblically speaking, is a person who wastes life. For God to call the rich man a fool is no minor insult.

So I have to ask, was God being fair? I mean, what made the rich man so foolish?

He made lots of money and saved lots money. Most of us would describe that kind of behavior as responsibly successful.

I think the answer is found in Luke 12:19: "And I will say to my soul, Soul, you have ample goods laid up for many years; relax, eat, drink, be merry."

For the rich man, life *did* consist in the abundance of possessions. He believed that because he had accumulated wealth, there was nothing left to do but eat, drink, and be merry. He bought into the lie that said because he had a lot of money, he wouldn't long for more. But God knew differently. God knew that no matter big his bank account was, it would never be big enough. That's just not how God created us. Things cannot satiate our hearts. Saint Augustine said it this way: "Our hearts are restless until they find rest in God."

Is your heart restless? Have you found rest in God? There is only so much time to do it. Don't forget; it's later than we think.

As time grew short for Paul, he had to make some decisions about his life. So he did. He finished his residency and became a brain surgeon. Then he and his wife had a baby—a baby he got to hold and kiss and love. And then he wrote his book because he knew his heart wouldn't be satisfied if he didn't. So he wrote and he wrote and he wrote until he needed morphine, until he could no longer write and kiss and love. And then, he left this world in peace.

Dr. Paul Kalanithi died at the age of 37.

As I write these words, I'm 34. I remember turning 19 and feeling sad that I was "getting old." I wish I could go back in time and tell that 19-year-old a thing or two. So now I'm 34. And my hair is falling out—I see it on my pillow when I wake up in the morning. And I feel the heat of the sun on my scalp in new ways. A few months ago I had to enlarge the font size on my phone in order to see it. And when I look in the mirror, I see lines and grooves in my skin that weren't there just a few years ago.

I am still very young, but there is a passing of time I can't deny. I—like you—am moving toward my death. And this scares the ever-loving you-know-what out of me.

I once heard pastor Matt Chandler preach in a sermon that most of us will be forgotten within one generation of our life. I bristled at that notion. *Nah*, I thought. *People will remember me. I'm important. I'll do great things.*

Chandler then asked the congregation for a show of hands from the people who knew the names of their grandparents and great grandparents. Most hands went up.

"What about great-great-grandparents?" he asked.

Very few hands went up.

We are but a breath, the psalmist says. Here today and gone tomorrow.

The good news is that today is not tomorrow. You are reading these words today. You are breathing air today. You are thinking and hoping and loving today. You are alive. So *be* alive!

I had the honor of watching my son, Charles, be baptized. He was five months old at the time—which is another way of saying he was perfect.

As I gazed at him during the sacred liturgy, I had an unexpected thought whirl through my brain. *You're going to bury me. If things go according to plan, I will grow old, and you will become a man. And then, when my days are done, you will put my body in the ground and commend my spirit back to God in a similar manner to how we have asked God's Spirit to descend upon you today.*

These thoughts did not fill me with sadness, only joy. They reminded me that I have a job to do and very little time to do it. I need to raise my son. I need to show him how to love God, love his neighbor, and live as a godly man. I have no time to waste.

Our lives are never really our own. They come and then they go. And this happens very, very fast. But what we have—all we have—is today. And there is no better version of today than a today lived for someone else.

We have been granted life. We must give that life to others.

May today be a day you *see* and *know* that you have the power to bring life to another.

You are not dead yet. Spread your life.

Today.

Because today is all you have.

i'm gonna bless you!

This entire commandment that I command you today you must diligently observe, so that you may live and increase, and go in and occupy the land that the Lord promised on oath to your ancestors. Remember the long way that the Lord your God has led you these forty years in the wilderness, in order to humble you, testing you to know what was in your heart, whether or not you would keep his commandments. He humbled you by letting you hunger, then by feeding you with manna, with which neither you nor your ancestors were acquainted, in order to make you understand that one does not live by bread alone, but by every word that comes from the mouth of the Lord. The clothes on your back did not wear out and your feet did not swell these forty years. Know then in your heart that as a parent disciplines a child so the Lord your God disciplines you. Therefore keep the commandments of the Lord your God, by walking in his ways and by fearing him. For the Lord your God is bringing you into a good land, a land with flowing streams, with springs and underground waters welling up in valleys and hills, a land of wheat and barley, of vines and fig trees and pomegranates, a land of olive trees and honey, a land where you may eat bread without scarcity, where you will lack nothing, a land whose stones are iron and from whose hills you may mine copper. You shall eat your fill and bless the Lord your God for the good land that he has given you.

Deuteronomy 8:1-10

If you haven't had the chance to be in the room when a brand new human arrives, I highly recommend it. It will change your life. Guaranteed. Just make sure you ask permission before showing up.

Before my wife gave birth to our first son, I struggled with the concept of miracles. I mean, why are some people miraculously healed from cancer while others are born with no legs and arms? Miracles have always seemed super unfair to me.

All that changed when my son was born. When I saw new life come into this world, my entire perspective on miracles changed. I now wake up every day expecting to see one. Doctors and nurses who work in labor and delivery might have the best gig in the world— except for being on call in the middle of the night.

It is hard to accept the premise that you know how the world works after you've seen a birth. It shatters your worldview. In. The. Best. Possible. Way. Before you've seen a baby come forth from her mother, you might believe that miracles don't happen often. Once you've seen new life emerge, you know the sacred truth. Miracles are all around.

When our second son Charles was born, I started thinking about the birth of our first son Ford, and how I had changed since becoming a father. And I don't mean my thinning hair or the fact that I now fall asleep every night thinking, *Brown bear brown bear what do you see?* When Ford was born, I was scared. I wanted to be a father—but I had never been one before. I had a lot of questions.

How do I change a diaper? What do I do if he won't stop crying? What if he doesn't like me? Some people don't!

And those were the easy ones.

I had much harder ones, like, *What if I'm not good at this? What if I can't make enough money? What if I can't answer his questions?*

Those were tough. But here are the questions that kept me up at night:

What if I can't meet his needs? What if I give him all I have—every ounce of my love and passion and money—and it's not enough? Then what?

Any other parents out there asking these terrifying questions?

When Ford was born, I stood frozen as nurses examined him. I stood there for about minute before I asked, "Can I touch him?"

"You're the father," the nurse said.

Oh, right. I crept forward and stuck out a single finger and touched his little leg. I'll never forget it. Total magic. I was his father, and he was my son. But I was still scared out of my mind.

Things were different the second time around. I didn't ask permission—I grabbed my son from the nurses as soon as my wife delivered him, and I made the sign of the cross on his body, blessing him in the name of the Father, Son, and Holy Spirit. Right there in the middle of the delivery room, I gave thanks to God for him.

That's what a blessing is. To bless is to thank. To thank is to bless. If you've ever said "thank you" or had it said to you, you know that thankfulness and blessedness are inextricably linked.

I thought about the relationship between the thanking and blessing a lot in the days following my sons' births. It's hard to not be thankful with a newborn in your arms.

Our lesson reflects this abiding sense of gratitude as well. The Israelites have wandered in the wilderness for years, and now Moses stands before them, recalling all they've been through and all God has done. Then he talks to them about a future he won't live to see. Moses will never enter the Promised Land. God has told him that. Moses understands that it is his fate to bring the people to the border of the Promised Land—and then fade away.

Can you imagine leading the Israelites all those years—only to be denied the fruits of your labor? That's a bitter pill to swallow. Even so, Moses speaks of blessing because he knows the people of Israel need to hear it. They have been through a lot, wandering lost in the desert, battling the temptation of idolatry, attacked by enemies. To put it mildly, the years have been hard.

But there has been good too. God has led the way, providing daily bread and offering protection when enemies attacked. Similar to our lives, the journey has been one of peaks and valleys. I often tell people that life is nothing but a series of highs and lows—it's always a mixed bag. There will be cursing, but there will always be blessing. We just have to keep our hearts and minds open to see them both.

I saw a bumper sticker recently that said, "Life is hard, then you die." And I have heard people say that the hardest years of our lives are the ones between ten and seventy.

Life is hard. It's good to say that out loud, to acknowledge that some days all we can see is the cursing. But the blessing is always there, because God is always there—no matter what.

On the same day our second son Charles was born, Andrew Quarless, a tightend for the Green Bay Packers, was preparing to welcome his daughter into the world. But the delivery didn't go as planned, and a day that should have been filled with joy wasn't. We took Charles home while the Quarless family laid their precious child to rest. As I read their story, I tried to feel their pain. I tried as hard as I could to crawl inside their grief, to understand what it would have been like to lose Charles.

But I couldn't. It was too awful—too hard. There my wife and I were, feeling nothing but blessing. And there the Quarless family was, feeling something very, very different.

The very next week, Mark Zuckerberg, billionaire and Facebook genius, announced that he and his wife were expecting a child. He also revealed they had suffered three miscarriages. "It's a lonely experience," Mark wrote on Facebook. "Most people don't discuss miscarriages because you worry your problems will distance you or reflect upon you—as if you're defective or did something to cause this. So you struggle on your own." He went on to explain, "in today's…connected world, discussing these issues doesn't distance us; it brings us together. It creates understanding and tolerance, and it gives us hope…We hope that sharing our experience will give more people the same hope we felt and will help more people feel comfortable sharing their stories as well."

I admire him so much for doing that, for continuing to mourn with those who mourn, even when they were now celebrating. To me, that's a perfect example of blessing in the midst of tragedy.

Blessing.

Cursing.

Good.

Bad.

Sadness.

Joy.

This is life.

Our challenge, Moses says, is to say thank you anyway.

To experience darkness.

To experience blessing.

And then to somehow look to God with a thank you on our lips.

We don't always want to thank God. At times, we'll want to curse God. And maybe we will. I certainly have.[1] But I've discovered in those moments of screaming at God that he is big enough to take it.

I've also learned that saying thank you when I don't want to say it helps me accept that I don't control what happens in this world.

God does. And the truth is that no matter what happens, there are countless reasons to give God thanks. This is what Moses is saying. He wants the people to bless God, even though life isn't all blessing. He says, *Enter the land. Take what God has given you and remember the ways he provided for you on the way in. Remember the manna you ate, the daily bread God fed you. Remember the clothing on your back and the shoes on your feet. Remember how God is bringing you to a land of milk and honey where you'll lack nothing. And do not forget, the Lord has never forgotten you. It's not been easy. It never is. Not for anyone. Bless God anyway. Say thanks anyway. Bless God, even when you don't want to.*

We practice this kind of blessing every Sunday in my church. After the first lesson is read, the reader says these words: *The Word of the Lord.* And the congregation replies: *Thanks be to God.*

Normally this is an easy thing to say. I like the Bible. And hearing from it often makes me happy. *Thanks be to God.* No problem. But I'm less grateful about other texts. Consider text like Zephaniah 1:17 where God says, "I will bring such distress on people that they

---

1 I'll never forget the first time I heard a man cuss during prayer. I was working at a Christian youth camp, and the director of the camp was praying aloud and he was really pouring out his heart to God. He was also really upset. Right in the middle of the prayer he dropped an S-bomb. My eyes shot immediately open. But he just kept on praying. That S-bomb taught me more about prayer than years of Sunday School.

shall walk like the blind; because they have sinned against the Lord, their blood shall be poured out like dust, and their flesh like dung."

Thanks…be to…God? I guess.

Blessing and cursing.

We can't escape it. Not even when we read the Bible. What we *can* do is trust the God who promises to see us through it. If you need help doing that today, heed the words of Moses.

Bless the Lord in all circumstances. Say thank you, thank you, and thank you—even on the way down. And remember that there is power in thank you.

During Charles' birth, Jenny was one of my wife's nurses. Jenny was three nights from retiring when we met. She had been a nurse for thirty-four years. She was eighteen and flipping burgers when she heard she could make double as a nurse's aide. "They trained you on the job back then," Jenny said. "So I jumped right in. When the day was over, I snuck back into every patient's room and asked if there was anything else I could do for them. I had never been so happy. As I rode the elevator down I told God, *Thank you. Thank you for showing me what to do with my life. Thank you.* From that moment, I never wanted to be anything but a servant. And let me tell you, thirty-four years later I can say God is good. He is so good. And I'm so thankful."

Jenny was crying. I was crying. Baby Charles was crying.

Thirty-four years as a nurse cannot have been easy. In fact, I suspect few jobs are harder than nursing.

"God is so good," Jenny said.

I bet there were nights when that was a hard thing to say. Nights on her knees with nauseated patients, panicked family members, the groaning of the dying. Thirty-four years of servanthood, and she's blessing the Lord. How does one do that?

We can start by reading this passage from Moses—and knowing, really knowing, what Moses knew: that no matter what happens, good or ill, God is leading the way. And though situations may be rough, you can trust that God will take you to a land of milk and honey—and give you bread along the way.

As a father, I try to lead my boys to milk and honey. I try. But I'll fail some days because I'm human and flawed. That is why it will be the joy of my life to tell them—as I tell you today—of a better Father, one who cannot fail, one who has no doubt as to whether or not our needs can be met, a Father who does not hesitate a second to grab our lives and bless them.

We have a trustworthy Father.

Today may we remember the love we have received, the clothes on our backs, and the shoes on our feet. May we trust in our daily bread, knowing that what was enough for the children of Israel is enough for us.

And may we lift our voices and say, *Thanks be to God!*

hungry

If there is among you anyone in need, a member of your community in any of your towns within the land that the LORD your God is giving you, do not be hard-hearted or tight-fisted toward your needy neighbor. You should rather open your hand, willingly lending enough to meet the need, whatever it may be.

Deuteronomy 15:7-8

Have you ever looked into the eyes of a hungry person? Ever watched someone dig through trash and then eat what they have found rotting there? Or maybe you've traveled to an impoverished country and hugged a child of skin and bones?

If you are reading this book, it probably means you've never had to miss a meal in your life. I could be wrong, but you are most likely among the people who go to sleep at night with their appetites fully satiated. This is nothing to feel ashamed of, but it is a privilege worth acknowledging. The reality is that 870 million people around the world won't have enough to eat tonight and will go to bed hungry—870 million of them. *Tonight.*

In Texas, the state I call home, one in six people live in poverty. That means their average income is around $11,000. If a household has two people, the poverty line jumps to sixteen grand. Most of us drive cars worth more than sixteen grand. Some of us have watches worth more than that! I'm not writing this to shame you. I *am* you. Well, I don't have a $16,000 watch, but I've got some really nice things. And I always have enough food. Always. The only time I don't eat is when I'm being a spoiled brat about the food not being good enough—or not something I like to eat.

I live in tremendous privilege. There's no other way to say it. I may not drive a Mercedes, but I own a car. That fact alone makes me richer than 92 percent of the world.

In my home state, one in five folks are food insecure[1], which means they don't have reliable access to a sufficient quantity of affordable, nutritious food. Nearly two million Texas children don't have regular access to food, and three million of them qualify for free or reduced-cost lunches in our public schools.

In other words, poverty and hunger aren't distant problems for *other* people. They are *our* issues—you and me—those of us who live in tremendous privilege.

Our lesson for today comes from a sermon by Moses. Actually, it's from his final sermon, which appears in the book of Deuteronomy. It's the longest sermon in the entire Bible. When Moses finishes giving it, he dies, because that's what happens when preachers preach too long.

Moses is talking about what is supposed to happen every seventh year when all debts are cancelled. Yeah, you read that right. All debts are cancelled. The Jubilee is a year of release when debtors

---

1   https://www.feedingtexas.org/learn/

are given the chance to re-enter society and the economy in viable ways. Later on, Moses reminds the people that if they don't like this teaching, they should remember when they were slaves in Egypt and God chose to set them free.

Give to the poor, Moses says. *Do it liberally, joyfully, without concern for what you'll get back. Set the people free. Give them life, just as God first gave it to you.*

I read those words, and they basically terrify me. So many people need help. I see them on street corners. They come up to my car window at stoplights. Sometimes my heart is soft and I give. But the honest-to-God truth is that most of the time my heart and hand stay closed, and I don't give. And, look—it's tough to say whether that's right or wrong of me, and we all know the reasons why. Some people say rewarding a panhandler only perpetuates problems, encouraging homeless people not to seek help from legitimate charities and shelters that could assist them in getting off the streets. Others say giving money to a homeless person could exacerbate an addiction by providing funds to buy drugs or alcohol.

I once knew a guy who regularly took a homeless man to the grocery store to buy him food—and sometimes liquor. Is that right? Debatable. I'm not sure I would do it. But my pal had a genuine friendship with that homeless man. How many of us can say that about the homeless people we see every day? I know I can't.

A few months back, I was walking into Barnes & Noble bookstore, and a man asked me for lunch money. I blew straight past him. I went in to look for a book, but my heart grew heavy. The Spirit began to move. So I went back outside and gave that man cash. I have no idea if he was hungry or looking to get high. But here's the question I've been chewing on: Does it really matter?

I'm not saying we should turn off our brains and give to every person who asks. Some people are wolves in sheep's clothing. But in this passage, Moses isn't telling us to make shrewd decisions about when to give. He is telling us to keep our hearts soft and our hands open. *Give freely*, he says. *Don't begrudge the poor—love them.*

We are never going to agree on the best way to feed the hungry, house the homeless, or support refugees. What matters is that we do these things—each of them in our own way. Recently Harvard University received the largest single donation in its history. Investor and philanthropist John Paulson gave $400 million to the school's existing endowment of $36.4 billion.

And author Malcolm Gladwell went bananas about this donation on Twitter.[2] Here's the recap:

> Gladwell's first tweet: "It came down to helping the poor or giving the world's richest university $400 mil it doesn't need. Wise choice John!"

> Gladwell's second tweet: "Next up for John Paulson: volunteering at the *Hermes* store on Madison Avenue."

> Gladwell's third tweet: "If billionaires don't step up, Harvard will soon be down to its last $30 billion."

Harvard psychologist Dan Gilbert tweeted a reply to Gladwell: "Cheap jokes and bad logic. If you want to end poverty, research and education are the best investments."

Entrepreneur Marc Andreessen also responded to Gladwell: "America's universities are a wellspring of progress and economic growth. Gifts to them are moral virtues, full stop."

---

2 http://www.businessinsider.com/malcolm-gladwell-goes-nuts-on-john-paulsons-harvard-donation-2015-6

These three very smart men disagree about how to best give to the poor. Reasonable minds have always—and will always—disagree on this issue. What matters is that reasonable minds *care* about this issue, because God cares about this issue. God cares deeply about the poor.

Jesus Christ has no earthly status. He has no privilege, no money, not even a place to lay his head. He lives as a very poor man. And this poor man tells us that whenever you and I feed the hungry, it is as though we have brought bread to his very lips.

So here's my question for you: Do you see the face of Jesus when you see the face of a poor person? I don't. Not always. But I want to. I want to stay soft. I want to stay open.

My father has had a long and successful career in the construction industry. And his success afforded my family some financial privilege while I was growing up. But construction is a volatile industry, and we experienced some lean years.

In third grade, my teacher said our class was collecting groceries for a family who could use a little help. She asked us to bring something back the next day. That evening I excitedly told my mother about our class project. I told her I wanted to help this family. My mother's eyes welled with tears. I don't remember what she said, but she sent me back to school the next day with food for the needy family. I was so proud to be helping!

It wasn't until I was an adult that I learned *we* were that family.

So stay soft, my friends. Stay open.

You never know who you are helping. The poor...
a friend...perhaps even the Son of God.

the hot mess of easter

They found the stone rolled away from the tomb, but when they went in, they did not find the body.

Luke 24:2-3

Facebook is funny. Some days I love it; other days, not so much.

You know how this goes.

I log onto Facebook and see a red notification that signals some new message or post. I think, *Ooh, something's happened. I better see what.* Then I click and discover I've been tagged in a photo. And I think, *a photo of me? I love photos of me. In fact, the only thing I love more than a photo of me is a photo of me on Facebook!*

But then I see the photo.

And I immediately dislike the friend who only moments before I adored. Why would she ever put *that* photo on the Internet? Facebook is the place where we showcase our perfect lives. And only photos that meet that standard should be shared. The one taken from our good side, the one from that expensive vacation, the one where the kids are smiling and the kitchen is spotless.

We live in a time during which we have the power to clean up our lives before we share them. So we do. Our lives are far messier than we let on, and yet we play the game. This isn't bad, in itself. There's nothing inherently wrong with putting our best feet forward. I always make sure to get a haircut before I preach on Easter Sunday— even if no one else would care about (or notice) my split ends.

The church puts on its best face too for Easter. We dress up the altar. We smile extra wide. Lutheran pastor Nadia-Bolz Weber says Easter is "the church's version of putting out guest towels."

Again, this isn't bad. It's Easter. Christ is risen! Death has been defeated. This is a party! It's good to get cleaned up for a party.

But recently I was reading the Easter story, and I was suddenly struck by how *not* cleaned up this story is. For a day on which we polish the silver and tuck in our shirts, the story itself is a total circus.

Compare Easter to Christmas. Now *that's* a cleaned-up story! Sure, Mary and Joseph take some licks, but by the time Jesus is born, they're a freakin' Norman Rockwell painting. Newborn in mother's arms, proud dad looking on, warm star above. Nice, clean, warm and fuzzy.

Easter, on the other hand, is a train wreck. Jesus is dead. Judas is dead. Peter has betrayed Jesus. And the rest of the disciples are AWOL. It's chaotic and confusing and sad. And if this isn't bad enough, nobody can get the story straight. *What the heck happened?* Depends upon whom you ask.

Luke says women come to the tomb. Two men in dazzling clothes appear and scare the crud out of them. "Why do you look for the living among the dead?" they ask. "He's not here, but has risen."

Mark says something similar—this time, with only one angel, but this angel is super scary too. John confirms Luke's version of two scary angels but adds that Jesus is also there, *alive*. He creeps up behind Mary Magdalene and wants to know why she's crying because *apparently* the Risen Jesus has a sick sense of humor. But Mary doesn't recognize him—she thinks he's the gardener. Talk about anti-climactic.

So what do we know for sure about Easter?

> *Only women are brave enough to come to the tomb.*

> *Angels are scary.*

> *Jesus isn't dead, though he might have some dirt under his fingernails.*

Easter is a hot mess of a morning. It's not the version we would post to Facebook. We would clean it up, provide consistent testimony, and make it a little easier to believe. But that's not what the gospel writers did. *Were there two angels or one? Was Mary alone or with other women?*

Apparently these details don't really matter. Something unimaginable, unthinkable has happened. Jesus, who died on a cross, has risen from the dead. This one fact is so unexpected that the disciples can't get anything else straight. Could you?

Mary, what happened?

Peter, what happened?

He's risen, they say. *He's risen.*

They can't explain it. So they don't even try. They know it is a mess. But it is the most beautiful mess they have ever seen. So they leave it messy.

Nobody claims to see the actual event. Have you ever thought about that? No one says: *I saw the resurrection! There was an explosion in the sky and BAM, Jesus came roaring to life!* No one says this. They say, *It happened when we weren't looking,* they say. *It happened in the dark. We didn't see it, but we've seen him. We've seen the Risen Lord.*

Some people struggle with the resurrection. I get that—I've struggled with it too. But the reality is that as much as we might want a cleaned-up Easter, it's good we don't get it. Two people—even two eyewitnesses—rarely recount an experience the same way. In fact, this usually only happens when people are lying.

When President John F. Kennedy was assassinated, thousands of people were watching the parade. The event was recorded on film. And yet it's one of the great American mysteries. What happened?

The president died. That we know for sure. Beyond that…uh, who knows? Historical truth is most often a collection of messy facts. But that doesn't make it any less true.

What is the truth of Easter? Our Lord rises from the dead. Beyond that…uh, who knows?

The truth is messy. Easter is messy. Jesus is dead. And then he isn't.

All the gospel writers say this. And billions of people, for two thousand years, have believed it. This is remarkable, because if there's one thing in life that's not messy, it's death. That's what makes death so brutal. When a person is gone, they're gone. And they stay gone.

I get annoyed when Christians rush to talking about resurrection in the shadow of death. I'm not supposed to say that. I'm a preacher and a Christian writer. My job is to tell you there is life beyond the grave—which there absolutely is. But in the moment of loss, you just want your loved one back. And you can't have him or her. And this is a loss that burrows into your heart, sucking out all the sun and light until you feel only the cold and dark.

Some pastors make it through their entire career without burying a child. I've done it twice. In consoling a mother who has lost her child, I've found that resurrection talk isn't all that helpful. She just wants her baby back. Can you blame her?

In Judaism, there's a custom called sitting *shiva*. When a person dies, the family sits shiva, which basically involves sitting together for a week. During shiva, friends are encouraged to come and sit with the bereaved family. The brilliance of shiva is that it requires no answers, only presence.

When you come to sit, you're not expected to say anything. If the grieving person wishes to speak, then he or she speaks. If not, then not. The purpose isn't to clean up death. The purpose is to grieve. Your presence, not your answers, is what matters most. When you sit shiva, you don't try to explain the mysteries and vagaries of death. You sit. Your presence says: *This is hard, my friend, but you are not alone.* It's the action, not the words, that matters most.

I think this is what the gospel writers understand when they give us their messy Easter stories. They know that explaining the resurrection isn't nearly as important as knowing it has happened. This is both the glory and trouble of Easter. The church still doesn't answer all our questions. Instead she sings of one great truth: Jesus Christ was dead and is risen.

And because of this great truth, we too may rise again into new life.

Easter is an unlikely story. It's the *most* unlikely story. It's messy. It's complicated, and it's hard to believe—like most of the truths I've ever heard.

A woman recently told me about the death of her husband. It was the end, she said, and he closed his eyes.

"Oh," he said. "I can see it."

"What?" the wife said. "What can you see?"

"An angel," he said. "Two of them."

"What else do you see?!"

He closed his eyes again, but this time he kept them shut. With total calm, he said, "You wouldn't understand."

And then he was gone.

We *don't* understand, do we?

Saint Paul says, "For now we see in a mirror, dimly, but then we will see face to face. Now I know only in part; then I will know fully, even as I have been fully known."

Until then, my friends, may we believe. May we enter into the mess of Easter and refuse to clean it up. May we stand with Mary and the disciples and be honest enough to say, *I can't explain this. I didn't see it happen, but one thing I know: What was dead now lives.*

For I've see what they said could not be seen.

I have seen the Risen Lord.

an
uncertain
trinity

I still have many things to say to you, but you cannot
bear them now. When the Spirit of truth comes, he
will guide you into all the truth; for he will not speak
on his own, but will speak whatever he hears, and he
will declare to you the things that are to come. He
will glorify me, because he will take what is mine
and declare it to you. All that the Father has is mine.
For this reason I said that he will take what is mine
and declare it to you.

John 16:12-15

Do you remember when your schoolteachers were
complete and total mysteries, mythical creatures who
came to life when the school bell rang each morning
and vanished at 3:30 p.m.? I remember seeing my third-
grade teacher in the grocery store and thinking, *She eats
food? Huh. That's interesting.*

In seminary, I had a professor who was a total mystery
to me. A former Jesuit priest, he'd been sent to Japan
to study Buddhism. After some time, however, my
professor began to identify with Buddhism as much
as he did with Christianity. Practicing Zen meditation
opened his prayer life in such unexpectedly beautiful

ways that he couldn't help but be drawn further into the religion. He was the first person I'd ever met who identified fully as both a Christian and a Buddhist. The notion that this was even a possibility was exotically attractive to me. But if I'm being honest, it was also kind of scary because it shattered my preconceived notions of what a religious person could or could not be. I'm not sure I ever understood this man, but I deeply respected him and learned something life changing from him: how to meditate.

"Sit upright," he would say. "Close your eyes and breathe. Take a deep breath in, push it out. Think of nothing but the rhythm of your own breath. When a thought enters your head, recognize it, and then push it away. Take another breath, thinking of nothing else. Now push it out."

We would follow his instructions for ten or fifteen minutes. Every. Single. Class. Have you ever tried to *not* think for fifteen minutes? It's hard. Like, really hard. I couldn't do it. Not at first. Honestly, I didn't want to do it. I thought it was a waste of time. If we had ten minutes to spare, then I wanted class to end early. I had other things to do.

But as the semester continued, I began to notice a change within myself. After meditating, my thoughts were clearer, my body calmer, my prayer life richer. I didn't understand it. I couldn't explain it. I just knew it was happening. I knew it was real.

This dual mystery of otherworldliness and certainty shapes how I talk about God. I can't ever fully explain God. What I know is that God is and God loves. Beyond that, how do I put God into words? Won't I always be leaving something out?

I wrote a paper in college titled *The Nature of God*. I handed it to the professor. He read the title and said, "Well…that's ambitious."

"Read it," I said eagerly. "I think I figured it out."

No. No. No. No. No! If I had a time machine, I would go back to that moment and apologize for being so incredibly näive. I did *not* have it figured out—not then, not now.

I have *some* understanding, sure, but I don't fully understand God because nobody does. Look, I don't even understand how airplanes fly. Seriously.

I have a basic understanding of lift and drag and am vaguely aware that some folks in the cockpit know what they're doing. But the truth is I fly by faith. I don't really understand how it works. And that's okay.

I know enough to trust.

Saint Paul writes in his first letter to the Corinthians: "Now we see things imperfectly, like puzzling reflections in a mirror, but then we will see everything with perfect clarity. All that I know now is partial and incomplete, but then I will know everything completely…"

We know, yes, but we know only in part. It's a humble kind of knowing, one that readily admits there's always more to know.

So what *do* we know about the nature of God? We know God as Father, Son, and Holy Spirit. We call this the Trinity, and we believe this to be a true doctrine. But—and this is a huge but—have you ever tried to explain the Trinity?

So God is one but has three names? Or is it three forms? Maybe it's three persons? Yeah, yeah, that's it! Three persons as one God. Or wait, I think there might be three Gods expressed in one form. Or is it the other way around?

See what I mean?

My professors talked about the Trinity a lot in seminary. I even read entire books dedicated to the topic. After years of study, I can distill what I learned down to one single sentence.

The Trinity is Mystery. This works for me because I love a good mystery. What I love most about mystery is not the solving of it, but rather *entering* into the mystery.

You see, God has revealed God's self to us, but God has not revealed to us all of God's self. We know, yes—but we only know in part.

One of the dangers of our time is that we have access to wide swaths of knowledge. The upsides are obvious. We get to know what our favorite celebrity looks like on vacation. We can search anything and come up with an answer (whether the answer is right is a different story). We can self-diagnose with the help of Dr. Google, and we run our own background checks on potential dates.

The downsides are more hidden. As a culture, we seem to believe that more information is always a good thing. But I'm not so sure it is. One of the problems I see with this perspective is that we often confuse certainty with understanding.

Before I married my wife, I was certain I knew what marriage was. Two people enter a lifelong covenant with God and each other. I was certain about the definition. Turns out that I actually had zero understanding of what marriage actually means. I had yet to live it—and some things, like marriage, can only be known through experiencing them. Wrestling with the doctrine of the Trinity is another one of these experiences. You can be certain about the words: God is Father, Son, and Holy Spirit, and never have a clue what they mean or how they relate to one another. Certainty is not understanding. Understanding is hard because it requires a willingness to live, explore, and ask questions. Ultimately, understanding requires a willingness to be comfortable with only partial knowledge. Our words are good, but they're never enough. God is three but also one.

I was at a conference for church leaders, and a man told a story about when his son was diagnosed with cancer. The father was watching over his son in the hospital when the pastor came for a visit. The father asked the pastor why God would allow his son to be so sick. The pastor replied, "It's not a good idea to do your theology in a hospital." I almost leapt out of my seat. *What!* I wanted to scream. *What do you mean the hospital is not a good place to do your theology? It's one of the best places!*

I understand what the pastor was trying to say—he wanted to remind the man that what was true about God before his son got sick was still true. This is an important point and not one to dismiss. What we declare on sunny Sunday mornings is still true during the dark of our stormy Friday nights. That matters. It does.

But if we can't honestly struggle with the nature of God in the midst of the messiness of our lives, then we'll never understand who God actually is. We can't understand the Trinity by reading a book or hearing a sermon. The only way to begin to understand the great mystery of God is by opening our lives.

> *We learn about God like Moses did—out in the desert.*
>
> *We learn about God like Daniel did—with lions at our throats.*
>
> *We learn about God like Jacob did—wrestling with an angel all night long.*
>
> *We learn about God like Job did—by losing everything.*

It's not a neat definition of God that matters most, but *experiencing* God as Father, Son, and Holy Spirit. It turns out the Trinity isn't so much a doctrine to be learned as it is a God to be experienced.

I know it would be easier if we worshiped a God who is one instead of three-in-one. Less confusing, for sure. More certainty would be involved. But then, there would be less understanding too. None of this is easy, but God has never been in the business of easy. God is too wrapped up in the business of our lives for that.

Years ago, I experienced a crisis of faith. It wasn't that I didn't believe in God. I just didn't think God cared about me. I didn't think God could hear—or wanted to hear—my prayers. It was about as low a feeling as I've had.

And one day, I went to church. I was numb. I sat through the worship music and the sermon in a deep state of loneliness. I felt utterly displaced. Church had always been my anchor, the place I could return to and trust to hold me steady when the waters got rough.

When it came time for communion, I decided to do something I had never done before in my life. I closed my eyes, bowed my head, and told Jesus I needed him to show up. *I need you right here and right now in the bread and the wine.* I told him I believed the bread was his body and the wine was his blood and that I desperately needed him more than anything in the world. And then I ate, and I drank.

And this moment changed the course of my life.

Because guess what? Jesus did what he said he would. He came. I didn't understand it. I couldn't explain it. I just knew it was real.

God is three
> *God is one*

What this means
> *Is God will come.*

the
smartest
man

They went to Capernaum; and when the sabbath came, he entered the synagogue and taught. They were astounded at his teaching, for he taught them as one having authority, and not as the scribes. Just then there was in their synagogue a man with an unclean spirit, and he cried out, "What have you to do with us, Jesus of Nazareth? Have you come to destroy us? I know who you are, the Holy One of God." But Jesus rebuked him, saying, "Be silent, and come out of him!" And the unclean spirit, convulsing him and crying with a loud voice, came out of him. They were all amazed, and they kept on asking one another, "What is this? A new teaching—with authority! He commands even the unclean spirits, and they obey him." At once his fame began to spread throughout the surrounding region of Galilee.

Mark 1:21-28

Church can be an awkward experience. Visitors arrive hoping to go unnoticed while simultaneously hoping someone will be friendly to them. They wonder where to sit and whether or not they're dressed appropriately. *Do people wear jeans to this church?* Some of the regulars sit down, say nothing, and stare at their shoes. Some wear jeans. Others don't. This does little to relieve visitors' anxiety.

Here's the most awkward thing I've ever seen in church: It's Easter Sunday in a large Baptist church, and we're sitting still, listening to the preacher. A woman a few rows behind us starts screaming. I do not mean a slight rising of the voice. I'm talking a battle cry, ferocious and gnarly. Every hair on my body stands up. I think a bomb is about to explode.

I whip around to see her standing, arms spread wide. She cries out, "It's about forgiveness! It's about resurrection! It's about new life! Today! Right now!"

And then, as if all of this was totally normal, she sits down.

The rest of us turn back to the preacher.

This is a tense moment. To his credit, the preacher handles it with grace. "Our sister is right," he says. "Today is *all* about new life. And I'm going to get there in just a moment. But as I was saying..." And then he sails on like a pro.

I've never forgotten that insanely awkward moment of disruption. Like most people brought up in church, I was taught to remain silent while the preacher preached. A person isn't supposed to interrupt church. When it's time for the sacred, it's also time for silence.

I imagine more than a few people are caught off-guard when the man with an unclean spirit from our scripture lesson bursts into the worship service.

Jesus is teaching to a spellbound crowd when this man cries out, "What have you to do with us, Jesus of Nazareth? Have you come to destroy us? I know who you are, the Holy One of God."

Can you imagine? This isn't awkward—this is frightening. The term "unclean spirit" was a common Jewish designation for a demon, which makes some of us squirm. I get that. Demons can be an unnerving topic. Some Christians are so uncomfortable with the discussion of demons that they simply pretend these passages of the Bible don't exist.

Others dismiss these passages, saying the ancient world blamed demons for people's various dysfunctions because they didn't understand mental illness. To a certain extent, this is probably true. No doubt, there was confusion about this topic, just like there still is today.

We live with a lot of stigmas around mental health and mental illness. We have a long way to go to understand that anxiety and depression are diseases just like diabetes and cancer. Some of us have them, others don't. The presence of mental illness has nothing to do with a lack of strength or character.

If you're dealing with any of this, I want you to know something: God is with you. And the church, while very flawed, is *behind* you and *for* you.

Okay? Read that paragraph again if you need to. Don't move on until you truly receive this message. The church has a bad track record on this issue. The good news is we're trying to repent.[1]

Okay, let's get back to the demons. The trouble with chalking up these demon scenes as a way to explain mental illness (or ignoring the passages altogether) is that there are too many of them. Mark is our oldest and probably most historically accurate gospel, and the brother talks a lot about exorcism. That means something.

---

1   I'm so serious about this issue that I have spent the last two years going to night classes to earn a master's degree in counseling. I believe the church needs more clergy who are also licensed mental health professionals, so we can not only better identify mental illness in our congregations but also understand how the church can be more helpful in supporting those seeking recovery from addiction, depression, anxiety, and other mental health challenges.

Later in the first chapter of Mark, we read, "that evening, at sundown, they brought to [Jesus] all who were sick or possessed with demons. And the whole city was gathered together. And he healed many who were sick, and cast out many demons."

In 2016, the world lost Marcus Borg, a brilliant New Testament scholar and fellow of the Jesus Seminar. Borg was a guy who really pushed the envelope, a true progressive. And while I didn't always agree with his views, he certainly made me think. He challenged me, and I'm sad he's gone. I bring him up now because Borg wasn't comfortable with miracles. He was the kind of guy who didn't like affirming too much what he couldn't explain. I can respect his position.

But when it comes to Jesus as exorcist, Marcus Borg believed. Of all the great healers in the Jewish tradition, more healing stories are told of Jesus than anyone else. The ancient historian Josephus described Jesus as a "doer of mighty deeds." Borg was fond of saying, "I don't understand it, but we can't deny that Jesus must have been a remarkable healer."[2]

These are powerful words from a skeptical, world-class historian.

So back to our story. Mark tells us it's the sabbath, and Jesus is in the synagogue, teaching. What's interesting is that we don't know what Jesus is saying, only that people are astonished, for he is teaching as one with authority and not like the scribes.

The scribes are teachers and lawyers who interpret scripture. What Jesus is doing is apparently different. He isn't just *appealing* to authority; he is *being* authority.

---

2   Marcus Borg *Meeting Jesus Again for the First Time: The Historical Jesus and the Heart of the Contemporary Faith* (San Francisco: HarperSanFrancisco, 1994) 31.

The man with the unclean spirit instinctively senses Jesus' authority and calls him out.

"I know who you are," he says to Jesus. "Have you come to destroy us?"

Jesus rebukes him, commanding, "Be silent, and come out of him!" And the unclean spirit, convulsing his body and crying with a loud voice, comes out. And the people are amazed.

Here's my question for us today: *Are we amazed?* Jesus has serious authority. But do we respect it? Are we amazed by it?

Authority is funny, isn't it? Some of us like it; some of us don't.

I went to a high school where the students wore uniforms. But there were special days when we didn't have to wear our uniforms, so-called "free dress days." On those days we were even allowed to wear hats, which I often did.

On one of these days, I walked into chapel wearing my hat. A teacher tapped me on the shoulder. "Ryan," he said, "take your hat off."

Without missing a beat I said, "Jews wear hats to pray."

Ooooooh, I would have slapped teenage me.

I confess to you this moment of my teenage idiocy to illustrate that I don't love being told what to do. But the older I get, the more I realize how much I need to be told what to do, because I don't always know what's best.

In the process of ordination to the priesthood, candidates are asked lots of questions about theology, the Bible, and personal life. Somebody asked me this question: *What does it mean for Jesus to be Lord and Savior of your life?*

I said, "He's my Savior because he saves me. Not just from sin and death but daily. He comes to me and rescues me. And he does it every single day."

That part of the answer came easy.

"He's my Lord," I said, "because I do things for him I don't want to do. I bow to his authority because I trust he knows what's best."

And as I said the words, I felt like a fraud, because for all my talk about Jesus as Lord, I try to control my own life and be my own lord.

But I need a Lord. Do you?

Here's the crux of the matter: We will never make Jesus our Lord unless and until we believe he knows more than we do. As my professor and philosopher Dallas Willard used to say, "It's not possible to trust Jesus, or anyone else, in matters that we don't believe him to be competent."

Would you fly with an incompetent pilot or let an incompetent surgeon perform a bypass? Do you give authority to anyone you don't believe is smart? I doubt it.

So the question becomes: Do you believe Jesus is smart?

We talk a lot about Jesus' grace, mercy, and love, but what about his competence? What about his ability to understand our lives?

Does he know how to help us be a good engineer? Can he help us parent our children or get an A in biology? Can Jesus appreciate the complexities of running a business or sustaining a marriage?

The earliest Christians believe Jesus knows this stuff. He is divine, which means he can't be dumb. That's why Saint Paul says Jesus holds all the treasures of wisdom and knowledge within himself

(Colossians 2:3). In other words, Jesus literally holds the world together—and keeps it running.

That takes a pretty impressive I.Q. Running the universe takes authority. To be totally honest, I think it's tough to claim Jesus as Lord until we're ready to claim he's really smart. And not just smart, but the smartest man who ever lived.

I was in a doctor's office some time ago having a routine physical. I had been going through a difficult time and was worried about my health. As the doctor was examining me my blood pressure shot up through the roof.

"Do you smoke?" the doctor asked.

"No."

"Drink?"

"Yeah."

"A lot?"

"Depends."

"On what?"

"Why don't you just take the reading again?"

He gave me a paternal look of worry and then took it again. Still high. That's when he did something interesting. He took the cuff off my arm, sat down and said, "Your father tells me you like to read."

"I do," I said, surprised.

"What do you read?"

I told him, and we started to talk about books and writing and running, even God. We carried on like this for nearly an hour. It was by far the longest conversation I've ever had with a doctor in an examining room.

At some point during the conversation, the doctor stood up, wrapped the cuff back around my arm and took the reading. "Ryan," he said, "you don't have a blood pressure problem. You have a stress problem. You're healthy." He smiled. "Relax."

So I did. And not just then but in the days that followed. The doctor's words had power in my life because I trusted his authority. I believed him to be competent.

We may not be demon possessed, but all of us, from time to time, get possessed by something—anxiety, money, guilt, regret.

Some force grabs hold of our souls, and we need the Lord to cast that force out. We need someone smart enough to understand the situation, someone who knows what to do. Someone who commands not only people but also spirits.

Don't be afraid to make Jesus your Lord. He won't abuse his authority—he will use it to set you free—from sin, from death, from demons, and even from yourself.

benedictus

Then his father Zechariah was filled with the Holy Spirit and spoke this prophecy: "Blessed be the Lord God of Israel, for he has looked favorably on his people and redeemed them. He has raised up a mighty savior for us in the house of his servant David, as he spoke through the mouth of his holy prophets from of old, that we would be saved from our enemies and from the hand of all who hate us. Thus he has shown the mercy promised to our ancestors, and has remembered his holy covenant, the oath that he swore to our ancestor Abraham, to grant us that we, being rescued from the hands of our enemies, might serve him without fear, in holiness and righteousness before him all our days. And you, child, will be called the prophet of the Most High; for you will go before the Lord to prepare his ways, to give knowledge of salvation to his people by the forgiveness of their sins. By the tender mercy of our God, the dawn from on high will break upon us, to give light to those who sit in darkness and in the shadow of death, to guide our feet into the way of peace."

Luke 1:67-79

I went to a small high school with a tradition of sending the senior class on a celebratory graduation trip. My class went to St. Petersburg, Florida. One night during the trip, about twenty of us went to see a movie. Afterward, we rode back to our hotel, ate dinner, hung out on the beach, and eventually wandered off to bed.

Around three in the morning, our chaperone received a call from the St. Pete police saying they had one of our students (we'll call him Walt) in a squad car. Apparently, Walt had fallen asleep during the movie and wasn't noticed by the cleaning crew—or *us* for that matter. So Walt just kept sleeping until he woke up around 2 a.m. (This was in the old days, before we all had phones in our pockets.) Walt tried to escape, but the theater doors were locked, and he tripped the alarm. That's when the cops showed up. Our chaperone corroborated the story with the police, and they released Walt into the chaperone's custody. The next morning, we all had a pretty good laugh at Walt's expense.

But this made me think. The chaperone counted our heads after the movie. Then we all ate dinner together and hung out by the water. During all of that time, nobody noticed Walt wasn't around. I couldn't help but wonder how that made Walt feel. He was missing, and nobody knew it. I wonder if he felt like nobody cared.

That image of Walt sleeping alone in a darkened theater, forgotten by those who were supposed to look after him, has never left me.

Have you ever felt like Walt? Like maybe God overlooked you? Ever waited so long for God to fulfill a promise that you felt as though God must have forgotten that he created you in the first place?

Our lesson in this chapter is a surprisingly hopeful song from a man who must feel forgotten by God. Zechariah is a priest in Israel during a time in which the nation hasn't heard from God in 400 years. The God who speaks directly to Moses, wrestles with Jacob, and inspires all the prophets, has gone totally and utterly silent. And his silence comes during a rough patch for Israel. It isn't like Israel is humming along in prosperity and peace, doing fine without the voice of God. Israel has repeatedly fallen into the hands of foreign powers and now finds itself under the brutal dominion of Rome. And still, God is silent. This is the world of Zechariah and his wife, Elizabeth. And yet Luke says they were righteous and blameless in the eyes of the Lord, even though their world is further complicated by infertility. Zechariah and Elizabeth are two people keeping the faith during a time of waiting on unfulfilled promises.

I think this is a place where many of us find ourselves today—living in that gap between promise and fulfillment, trying to keep our faith night after night, looking for tender mercies of God and the dawn that Zechariah promises. These are beautiful promises. We want them to be true—but are they?

A life of faith requires the ability to wait on God. For many, this is reason enough to turn away from God. Many are unwilling to yield authority to God unless he's like a vending machine, providing immediate response with the punch of a button.

I get that. Waiting sucks.

I had a friend who once fasted for forty days. He was in a tremendously dark period of life (like Israel) and needed deliverance. So he came up with a dangerous plan. He would fast for forty days to force God's hand. God would look down, see his superhuman act of spirituality, and be compelled to respond. So for forty brutally long days, my friend fasted, consuming nothing but water.

"So what happened?" I asked. "What did you learn?"

"Not a damn thing," he said.

"You didn't learn anything?"

"I learned God doesn't work that way."

"That's it?" I asked.

"That's it."

We can't force God's hand, can we? This is gut-wrenching because in the vacuous silence, another voice begins to whisper to us. It says, *God forgot. God doesn't care. There's no answer, no voice, no God coming to save you. There is nothing worth waiting for.*

A famous psychology experiment was performed in the 1960s called the Marshmallow Experiment. Experimenters placed children in a room and gave them a treat, a marshmallow or a cookie, with the following deal attached. The subject could eat the treat right away, or wait a few minutes until the experimenter returned. If the subject waited, he or she would receive two treats.

The documentary footage of the experiment is awesome. The children (who don't know they're being watched) fight hard against the temptation to eat the treat. Some cover their eyes with their hands; others turn around so that they can't see the treat. Another kid strokes the marshmallow like a beloved pet. One boy looks around the room to make sure nobody's watching. Then he picks up the proferred Oreo, twists it apart, licks the cream filling, puts the cookie back together, and returns it to the tray.

The psychologists followed the subjects as they grew into adulthood and discovered that those who waited were more successful in life. They had higher SAT scores and fewer behavioral problems. A follow-up experiment was performed recently. Again, researchers took a group of children and put each of them in a room alone—but this time with paper and a box of dull, used crayons. They told them they could either color with the used crayons or wait for a box of new ones. For half the kids, the experimenters kept the promise and brought in new crayons. For the other half, the researchers came back and said, "Sorry, we actually don't have any new crayons."

Then they ran the Marshmallow Experiment with the same subject group.

Guess how many kids from the group who didn't get new crayons waited for the second treat in the Marshmallow Experiment?

One.

The kids who had been burned in the crayon experiment no longer believed there was anything worth waiting for, so they didn't wait.

When my mother was a young girl, she wasn't sure there was much to wait for either. She never had the chance to meet her father because he drank too much and…you know how those kinds of stories go. Her mother was a good woman, but she had her own issues that made raising a daughter alone too difficult a task. For the first twelve years of my mother's life, she was passed between relatives. Listening to her describe what it felt like to believe nobody wanted her, that she had been forgotten, that there was nothing worth waiting for, is beyond painful.

Do we believe there's anything to wait for? Most of us, in some way, are the children who got burned in the crayon experiment. Most of us, on some level, are my mother. We want to know if there's anything worth waiting for. We want to know if somebody loves us.

We want to believe there's something worth waiting for, that God hasn't forgotten us, but promises have been broken in our lives. Spouses have left. Parents were absent. A loved one became violent. An employer lied. And that little whisper starts up again: *There's nothing worth waiting for. Don't get your hopes up. You'll get burned. You'll be forgotten. Again.*

Israel hasn't heard from God in 400 years, and then an angel tells Zechariah his wife will bear a son filled with the Holy Spirit who will turn the children of Israel toward God. But Zechariah is skeptical.

He has waited a long time, so he questions the angel. The angel says, *Don't believe me? Fine. You'll be unable to speak until the day these things occur.*

Zechariah has waited his whole life for a word from God and now he has one, but he is forced right back into a time of waiting (and a silent one, at that!) Elizabeth becomes pregnant, nine months of silence pass, and the child whom the world will know as John the Baptist is born. And finally, Zechariah speaks.

You can read Zechariah's words in our lesson. These are the first words that roll off his tongue after a long silence. Nothing can bring out our true colors like a good, long wait. When we wait, we can lie to others about how we feel. We may even lie to God in our prayers. But we can't lie to ourselves. If we're bitter, we know it. If we've lost hope, we know it. If our unanswered prayer consumes us, we know it. In waiting, we cannot run from ourselves.

Zechariah has waited literally his whole life to hear from God. So what does Zechariah say when he finally speaks? Two things. He remembers the past and then looks, with hope, to the future.

First Zechariah thanks God for all God has done. He recalls God's mercy, the revelations to the prophets, and how God has delivered Israel from its enemies. While Zechariah has been waiting in silence, his mind has wound back through time, considering the past mercies of God.

When you wait, where does your mind go? Do you obsess over what you don't have or do you thank God for what he's already given?

Isn't it strange how quickly we forget our blessings? One brutally effective spiritual discipline is to compare the amount of time we spend asking God for something versus the time we spend thanking God after it's been given. I confess: I spend months asking for something, only to receive it, offer one passionate prayer of thanksgiving, and move on.

This is why the repetition of liturgy and worship are so important. Truth can't be heard just once. If we want any real chance of remembering something, we can't hear it only once. Or even twice. In most cases, we need to hear the truth every single day. The human condition is that we are forgetful. This is why we return to the same prayers, the same liturgy, and the same promises. We need them again and again.

Sometimes I feel anxious, and the anxiety affects my sleep. I've discovered, however, if I recall all I am grateful for and how I have seen God's provision in my life, this remembering slows my brain, calms my soul, and carries me into sleep.

There is power in remembering. Thanking God for our many blessings drowns out the whisper of *you've been forgotten*. We must remember God's mercy on us in the past to sustain us in the present. God didn't forget you then, and God has not forgotten you now.

After Zechariah remembers, he looks with hope to the future. Why? He and his people have been living with unfulfilled promises for hundreds of years. What makes him so hopeful?

The angel says Zechariah's son will be the prophet of the Most High and give knowledge of salvation to his people. None of this has happened yet, but Zechariah looks to what God has promised and rejoices because God has a plan for his son's life. And he trusts that God is going to follow through on that plan.

God has a plan for you. He made you with a purpose and put a unique calling on your life that *only you* can accomplish. You are God's child, and there isn't another one of you. Only you can do what God has made for you to do. Pause and consider that for a moment: *Only you can do what God has made for you.* It's a marvelous thought—each one of us has a depth of value we can't even begin to comprehend.

I know what some of you are thinking: *You don't know my life. You don't understand how hopeless my job is, or my family situation, or my finances.*

You're right. I don't know what it's like to walk in your shoes. I don't know what it's like to feel your pain.

Here's what I do know: The mission to which God calls John the Baptist—to prepare the way of the Lord—is the same one to which he calls you. Jesus says we are to be his presence in the world. We are to be his hands and feet. We are to prepare the way of the Lord for a hurting world.

This is why Zechariah's song is our song. God wants us to be the light for those who sit in darkness, to guide our feet into the way of peace, to be the dawn breaking on high for someone in a dark place of pain.

You have been created to help usher in the kingdom of God, and nobody can do that for you. Sometimes life can feel so dreary that there doesn't feel like there's anything special to wait on. What is more exciting than partnering with God to bring a little mercy into the lives of those around you? What could be more purposeful than preparing the way of the Lord?

God made you for this. Don't miss it.

When my mother turned twelve, her aunt Rachel (who I would come to know as MeeMaw), said, "Enough. You're mine." She adopted my mother as her own.

The Lord has a great plan for my mother's life. She has traveled through some rough years to get there, but God has never forgotten her. She still has so much to wait for.

If you feel like my mother did—forgotten, unloved, abandoned—I want you to hear the voice of God through my Meemaw. "You're *mine*. I'll take *you. I want you.* I love you."

Zechariah says his son will prepare the way of the Lord.

May you join Zechariah today in remembering all God has done and will do in your life. May you reaffirm the ancient truth of the prophets and of Jesus himself.

You are loved.

You have not been forgotten.

And that for which you wait will be worth it.

stranger danger

Which of these three, do you think, was a neighbor to the man who fell into the hands of the robbers?" He said, "The one who showed him mercy." Jesus said to him, "Go and do likewise."

Luke 10:36-37

I've heard of preachers who avoid the parable of the Good Samaritan for their entire careers out of fear of having nothing new to say about this beloved story. That's not an issue for me—I don't live under the illusion that I *ever* have anything new to say! It may be ill-advised, but I'm going to write about the most famous parable in the Bible. Besides, I figure talking about our faith isn't so much about being the first to discover some new concept or idea, planting a flag as if it were my territory to claim, as it is about returning to something old and discovering something anew.

As a child, I was instructed to answer the telephone in a very formal manner. "Hello, this is the Waller residence, Ryan speaking. May I ask who is calling?"

It was a great scandal when my younger sister began answering the phone with a simple, "Who is it?" She had a deep, raspy voice, which made her blunt question even more awesome. People thought my parents had hired a chain-smoking bail bonds receptionist to answer our phones. Our parents were mortified.

I thought it was hilarious and didn't see what the big deal was about how my sister answered the phone. Now that I'm older, I understand my parents were attempting to teach us to welcome guests with warmth, on the phone and at our door. How we treat people matters. But the biblical concept of hospitality runs much deeper than mere pleasantry. The word hospitality, as it appears in the New Testament in Greek is *koine,* which literally means love of the stranger.

Fear of the stranger comes far more naturally to us—at least it does for me. Just the other night, I pulled up to a stop sign and saw a homeless man begging for change. Instead of rolling down my window and offering some cash, I locked my doors and looked the other way. It's shameful for me to admit that. But it's the truth.

The Old Testament commands us to love our neighbors as ourselves exactly once. But at least thirty-six passages of scripture tell us to love the stranger. Guess which message God doesn't want us to forget?

But we don't always want to love the stranger, and maybe that's not totally our fault. As children, what word do we learn to associate with stranger? Danger!

Stranger Danger! We teach our kids this rhyming warning because we don't want them to be kidnapped or hurt by a stranger. And while the sentiment is noble, perhaps the unintended consequence is that the phrase plants fear in our hearts toward those who look and sound different than we do.

Who do you fear? Of whom are you suspicious? Who does your heart naturally seem to reject? It's tough to admit that we think and have these feelings. We don't want to believe we feel this way toward any people. But we do. I locked my car door. Did that homeless person really represent danger, or did I respond in fear because of my own preconceptions? Probably the latter.

The first step in reversing our stranger-danger mentality is to admit that we see strangers as dangerous. Psychologists describe this process as becoming aware of our biases. Biases are like bacteria—you can't avoid them but becoming aware of them can help you avoid being made sick by them.

Once upon a time, a kid in my church youth group was cruel to me. He would swat at the back of my head during Sunday school and then cough underneath his breath, "Dandruff." My stomach still clenches when I think about the ways he bullied and embarrassed me.

One Sunday night at church, after we had returned from youth camp, he shared his testimony. He said that he had encountered Jesus. In front of our little church, he confessed that he hated black people. "I'm a racist," he said, tears streaming down his cheeks. "But I don't want to live this way any longer. I met Jesus. I can't live this way any longer."

I never liked that kid. He may have stopped hating black people, but he never liked me much. Still, his moment of courage struck a begrudging chord in me; hatred isn't an easy thing to admit feeling. But unless we first admit that hatred exists, we stand no chance of stamping it out of our lives. I need to know that my hands are dirty in order to feel compelled to wash them before dinner. Likewise, I need to search my heart for the people I hate, so I can do the work of transforming hatred into love.

Hating someone is a genuinely awful thing to do. But hatred is the key to understanding the parable of the Good Samaritan. In the story, Jews and Samaritans hate each other. They have no problem stating this fact. These two groups of people really, truly, genuinely, supremely hate each other. They take turns burning each other's temples to the ground. That's about as bad as things can be.

Recently the United States has experienced a spate of arsons at historically black churches. What a horrendous thing to do! To walk into a sacred space and torch it to the ground must be driven by hatred. How else could someone act out in such a grievous way? Hate has the power to encourage us to do things to other people that are otherwise impossible to imagine. Hate is a superpower gone wrong.

By the time Jesus tells this parable, the Jews and Samaritans have hated each other for about a thousand years. We trivialize this story if we don't take that fact seriously.

The Gospel of Luke shares Jesus' words:

"Teacher?" a lawyer says to Jesus. "What must I do to inherit eternal life?

"What is written in the law?"

"Love the Lord your God with all your heart, and with all your soul, and with all your strength, and with all your mind; and your neighbor as yourself."

"You have given the right answer," Jesus says.

"And who is my neighbor?"

A man was traveling alone, Jesus says, *when thieves came upon him. They stripped him, beat him, and left him to die. A priest came along but did nothing to help. Then a Levite saw the wounded man but also turned away. That's when a Samaritan (a bottom feeder, a stranger) looked upon the dying man with compassion. He bound his wounds, carried him to shelter, and paid for his care. Which man was the neighbor?*

"The one who showed him mercy," the lawyer replies.

"Go and do likewise."

Powerful story. But we've heard it a million times. So we trivialize it a million ways. We trivialize the priest and the Levite, dismissing them both as callous religious men who care nothing for a dying soul.

But of course they care. They may hate Samaritans, but surely they experience sorrow over the man's pain. One of the more beautiful things about humanity is our innate reaction to another's suffering. We turn toward one another's pain. We run into the flames. We jump into the water. We put our mouths on a stranger's and breathe. And we do all of this *without* thinking.

The priest and the Levite see the naked man; they hear his groans. They know what they are supposed to do. And I bet they wrestle with it. I bet it turnd their stomachs. I bet it keeps them up *all night long. Feel* their guilt. *Know* their sin of failing to act, of letting their hatred trump love. Jesus doesn't even mention the sin of the thieves who beat the guy and left him in the ditch to die. In the gospel, sin is often not attributed to obvious wrongdoers but rather to those who don't bother to love.

Jesuit priest and theologian Fr. James Keenan says we too often associate sin with weakness. "But in scripture, sin resides not so much in our weaknesses but in our strengths."

This strength is the sin of the priest and the Levite: They are in a position to do something—to help—and they do nothing. So often we religious people take potshots at obvious sinners like murderers and thieves. But in this parable, we see that Jesus is more concerned with the strong heart that does not bother than by the weak heart that struggles to love.

It is easy not to bother with the stranger, even easier to not bother with the stranger we hate. Is there someone you can't be bothered to love? A stranger you won't help? Re-read this parable and ask yourself those questions. Then consider how we trivialize this parable in another way too. We whitewash the Samaritan. *Isn't he sweet? What a swell guy. I wouldn't have gone so far as the Samaritan, but I'm glad he helped so much.*

This caricature isn't an honest assessment either. It doesn't reflect the deep and abiding love the Samaritan has for the stranger. Consider that the Samaritan knows he is helping a man who probably wouldn't do the same for him, a man who—had the tables been reversed—might leave him to die. He shows compassion anyway. He loves the stranger. He practices hospitality.

This isn't a Republican being nice to a Democrat—this is laying down your life for a person who doesn't care about yours. This is loving Bernie Madoff after he has stolen your life savings. This is praying for the bigot who persecutes you or your beloved or your babies.

This is no trivial, saccharine-sweet passage—this is radical, world-changing. You want to know what hospitality is really about? This. Loving people even when the world says to hate them.

Who is my neighbor? the lawyer asks Jesus.

Wrong question, Jesus answers.

The brilliance of the Good Samaritan is that he never asks whether or not the dying man is his neighbor. He just sees a stranger who needs help.

Neighbor isn't a term of limited liability. It's not about figuring out who we can neglect, which is what the lawyer is asking. The lawyer wants a point of clarity: Tell me who I don't have to worry about.

Nobody, Jesus says. *They all matter. You should worry and love them all.*

The great pacifist and advocate Martin Luther King Jr. put it this way: "The priest and the Levite ask, 'If I stop to help this man, what will happen to me?' But the Good Samaritan says, 'If I do not stop to help this man, what will happen to him?'"

Not stranger danger, but love of stranger.

Jesus never has the chance to practice our version of hospitality. The Bible says he has no place to lay his head, which means Jesus has no home in which to welcome friends or strangers. But that doesn't mean he isn't hospitable. Instead, Jesus takes hospitality on the road, making friends of strangers as he goes.

Sometimes this makes people nervous, just like it continues to do today. Radical love for an enemy shocks us. But Jesus does it. Others have done it.

During the Civil War, Abraham Lincoln was criticized for not being harsh enough with Confederate soldiers. One time, after a battle, a Union general asked why the troops hadn't destroyed the Rebel enemies. Lincoln said, "Do I not destroy my enemy by making him my friend?"

Not too long ago, a mother stood in a courtroom and faced a young man who had stolen her son's life. You might remember the story from the news—a man walked into a church and killed nine people who were attending a Bible study.

The mother looked at the young man and said, "We welcomed you Wednesday night in our Bible study with open arms. You have killed some of the most beautifulest people that I know. Every fiber in my body hurts, and I will never be the same. Tywanza Sanders is my son, but Tywanza was my hero. [He] was my hero. But as we say in Bible study, we enjoyed you. But may God have mercy on you."[1]

And she meant it. Watch the video. She meant it.

"Which of the three," asks Jesus, "was a neighbor to the man?"

"The one who showed him mercy," the lawyer says.

"Go and do likewise."

---

1   https://www.theguardian.com/world/2015/jun/19/hero-charleston-church-shooting-mother-shielding-others

one

There is no longer Jew or Greek, there is no longer slave or free, there is no longer male and female; for all of you are one in Christ Jesus.

Galatians 3:28

John Claypool was a Baptist preacher turned Episcopal priest who, among many other noble endeavors, was involved in the Civil Rights Movement. In his book, *The Hopeful Heart*, he tells the story about the time he and a rabbi participated in a tense meeting with several African-American ministers. The meeting ended with Claypool and the rabbi being accused of having no courage. Claypool said, "What started as a hopeful endeavor ended in total frustration." As Claypool left the meeting, he said to the rabbi, "I think it's hopeless. This problem is so old, so deep…there's no way out of it."

The rabbi had lived through the Holocaust. He replied to Claypool, "To the Jew, there is only one unforgivable sin, and that is the sin of despair…Think of the times you've been surprised…as you looked at a situation and deemed it hopeless. Then, lo and behold, forces that you did not even realize existed broke in and changed everything...If God can create the things that *are* from the things that *are not* and even make dead things come back to life, who are we to set limits on what that kind of potency may yet do?"

Have you ever committed the sin of despair? Maybe you weren't accepted to your dream school or were fired from your job. Maybe your spouse walked out. Whatever it was, you were convinced your life was over, and hope was nowhere to be found.

In 2016, we had the worst mass shooting in the history of the United States at a gay night club in Orlando, Florida. The victims were specifically targeted as members of the LGBTQ community (lesbian-gay-bisexual-transgender-queer). After the shooting, one of my gay friends said, "I failed at hope today."

Yeah, I thought. *I can understand why.*

I went to bed a few nights that week feeling this way too. I stirred under the light of the moon, feeling dread, feeling unwell, angry, confused, and very, very sad. I can't even imagine how my LGBTQ brothers and sisters must have felt. I can't imagine how they *still* feel. This was not simply a terrorist attack. This was a mass shooting aimed at gay people. Period. To say it any other way is to invalidate the suffering the members of the LGBTQ community face in this country.

There's a story in Mark's Gospel that is relevant to what's happening right now in America. You might remember it. This guy is paralyzed, and his friends really want to get him to Jesus because they believe Jesus can heal him. So they take him to the house where Jesus is, but so many people are there that they can't get in. But they don't despair. They climb onto the roof, cut a hole in it, and lower their buddy down to Jesus. What a glorious image! Friends who will stop at nothing to make sure their pal gets the healing he desperately needs. I love it.

This story may have been recorded almost two thousand years ago, but I can't think of one more appropriate for today. We are living in a time when we must carry one another and make sure everyone finds the healing they need, even if we have to climb up on roofs and cut holes in them to make it happen.

For a week after the shooting in Orlando, I watched images on television of the wounded being carried hurriedly into the streets, fleeing the nightclub where the shooting took place. I watched, in horror, as a mother wept openly to a reporter, unaware whether her son was dead or alive. Then I watched her weep again days later when she learned he had been killed.

This is not the time for debate. This is a time to cut holes in roofs so our friends can get to Jesus because we know that healing takes place at his hands and his feet. And since we've been commanded to *be* Jesus' hands and feet, we better get to it. There is no better way to do that than by loving one another.

In the wake of the Orlando shooting, many people rushed into a debate about sexual ethics and gun control. What I wish had happened is that we had taken some time to simply mourn, be silent, and then ask how we might help one another heal.

Sometimes I think we Christians forget that our first responsibility is not to debate one another but to allow Jesus' love to flood our hearts and minds so that we might go and love our neighbors. *All* of our neighbors.

Saint Paul writes to the people of Galatia, saying that in Jesus Christ, "there is no longer Jew or Greek, there is no longer slave or free, there is no longer male and female; for all of you are one."

It sounds nice, really nice. But when a crazed gunman bursts into a gay nightclub with an assault rifle and indiscriminately sprays bullets, killing forty-nine people, I have trouble believing we will ever live as one.

Our country is filled with hate, and the Christian experience is rife with division. At times it seems as though we are everything *but* one. We attack each another, we ridicule, we alienate, we fear, and we hate. And then, some of us even kill our neighbors.

But Saint Paul says it ought not to be so among those in Christ. In Christ, we become children of God. When we are baptized in Jesus' name, we are clothed in his very nature and bound together as one. In other words, there is no *you*. There is no *me*. There is only *us*.

What does that mean? Does it mean our differences don't matter? Does it mean we pretend that Jew and Greek, male and female, are exactly the same?

No. Of course not. Christianity doesn't ask us to erase our individuality—as if that were even possible. Our faith asks us to recognize that our unity is more important than our individuality. It asks that we die, daily, to ourselves so we may rise to new life—true life—in Christ Jesus our Lord.

But this transformation will never happen unless we take our true identities seriously. We are children of God, brothers and sisters through our faith in Christ. Nothing runs deeper than this—not a label we ascribe to ourselves nor any given to us by others. We are, by the loving grace of God, his precious and beloved children.

God sees Christ in you. Did you know that? This means you should see Christ in yourself—and in other people. Once you start seeing from this divine perspective, everything changes. Fr. Richard Rohr, a Catholic priest, says, "From this most positive and dignified position, you *can* let go of and even easily admit your wrongs. You are being held so strongly and so deeply that you can stop holding onto or defending yourself. God forever sees and loves Christ in you; it is only we who doubt our divine identity as children of God."

Believing this allows you to be filled with God's love and enables you to forgive and love yourself, which empowers you to love and forgive others—especially those with whom you disagree. This is what Christians do.

Jesus never sugarcoats his welcoming of people. He tells sinners not to sin, sure, but only after he embraces them, loves them, and becomes their friend. He never worries about being associated with the so-called wrong people, with prostitutes and tax collectors. He doesn't care about his reputation. He cares about salvation, and he wants everyone to have it.

Do you remember that dust-up between the Chick-fil-A restaurant chain and the LGBTQ community? The president of Chick-fil-A has a sincerely held belief about traditional marriage that it should be reserved for one man and one woman. It is his right to believe this. Because of this belief, a gay activist organized a boycott against Chick-fil-A. (As an aside, the president and gay activist have since become good friends, but that's another story about what happens when we dare to look past labels, treat one another with civility, and see the Christ in the other.)

You probably also remember that Chick-fil-A is always closed on Sundays. It's a company-wide policy. But on the day after the shooting in Orlando—a Sunday—Chick-fil-A brewed gallons of tea and prepared hundreds of sandwiches and handed them out for free to people donating blood to the victims.

No debate. No parsing of opinion. Just love.

People have differences, and these differences matter. But they don't give us an excuse to withhold love. To love as God loves is to love all of creation. God loves his enemies. And you know who God's enemies are, right?

Us. You and me. It sounds harsh, I know, but the Bible teaches that our sins make us enemies of God because sin makes us imperfect and God is perfect. Our sin separates us from God. But this is where things gets interesting. Instead of opposing his enemies, God does something completely different.

God stretches out the arms of love, and he dies for his enemies. For us.

In the letter to the Romans, Paul says, "For if while we were enemies, we were reconciled to God through the death of his Son, much more surely, having been reconciled, will we be saved by his life."

In our sin, we alienate ourselves from God. Jesus' response to that sin is to pour out his life for us. What he asks is that we do the same for one another.

There was and still is a lot of anger and blame going around since the Orlando shooting. It is easy to get caught up in blame. It makes us feel better to feel angry and point the finger at someone. My challenge to you is to heed Fr. Rohr's advice: Take the divine perspective by looking for Jesus in the faces of your brothers and sisters as Christ does. This is the only antidote I know for despair. We cannot, must not despair. It is okay to feel hopeless from time to time. But it is not okay to *remain* hopeless, because humanity, while deeply divided, is ultimately stitched together by love, not hate. When hatred seeks to rip us apart, God always re-sews in love. Always.

We saw this re-making in the weeks following the Orlando shooting. In the midst of tragedy, there were bright moments, as there always are when hatred rears its ugly head. Love fights back. It always does, and love *always* wins.

One way that love wins is through mourning. We must wrap our arms around the LGBTQ community and love them through this awful ache. They are scared right now. The worst mass shooting in history targeted them. How would you feel? I would be terrified. I would feel pushed to the edge of society and very vulnerable.

Jesus spends his entire ministry focusing on the vulnerable people. He goes painfully out of his way to ensure that those who feel neglected, downtrodden, and cast aside know of his love.

It is not the church's job to tell you what to believe about every social issue—sexual ethics. gun control, abortion. These are complicated issues with no easy answers. I won't—and the church shouldn't—tell you what to believe. The church's job—and my job—is to declare to you the love of Christ.

And that in Christ, there is no longer Jew nor Greek. Slave nor free.

No male.

No female.

Just children.

Children of a living, loving God bound together as one. May we go forth and treat one another as God always intends—as brothers and sisters—children of a most merciful Father who hears our cries in the dark of a bloody night and always,
always, always comes running.

that time
i needed
therapy

When Jesus heard this, he said to them, "Those who are well have no need of a physician, but those who are sick; I have come to call not the righteous but sinners."

Mark 2:17

A famous pastor in my city recently told his congregation that Christians shouldn't see professional counselors. Instead, he said they ought to rely on ministers and other church leaders for their psychological and emotional needs. His basic argument is that Christians should do *everything* in community. As such, the confidentiality that exists between therapist and client is un-Christian because it prohibits communication.

I'll give you a hypothetical. Let's say I tell my therapist I'm addicted to gambling, and I want help in breaking the addiction. The problem—according to Pastor Famous—is that my therapist needs the ability to inform my community about my addiction so they can be involved in my recovery. The laws of confidentiality prohibit my therapist from doing this. So this pastor concluded that Christians shouldn't go to therapy.

I'm not interested in shaming this pastor—his church does a tremendous amount good for the people of Dallas. But his remarks are dangerous because they undoubtedly keep people in his congregation from seeking out the help they need. I feel particularly strongly about this issue because I'm a Christian leader who has also found healing on a therapist's couch.

There are many things to worry about these days: gun violence, climate change, the seeming dearth of morality in American politics. But we also have much to celebrate. We are experiencing, I think, the burgeoning of a society that lauds honesty. Don't misunderstand me: We're still a long way from actually being honest with one another. Log on to Facebook to discover how much we prefer "sharing" our perfect moments and neglect those imperfect ones.

But we *value* honesty. We praise those who we believe are living authentic lives. In other words, we may not yet be honest, but we really, really want to be. It's a start.

Why do I bring this up? For too long, Christians struggling with mental health issues have been forced to struggle in silence. The time for silence is over.

Let me tell you a story. A woman called me at home. A friend suggested she listen to one of my sermons online, so she did. Now she wanted to talk. There was a tremor in her voice when I answered. Just making this call was a big deal for her. She wasn't accustomed to asking for help.

"In your sermon…" she began slowly. "You said having anxiety doesn't necessarily mean your faith is damaged. Is that right?"

"That's right," I said.

"Well, I'm struggling with that."

"Tell me about it."

She told me about the nighttime because that's when her anxiety was worst. She was a lawyer and a proud mother of three. During the day she functioned remarkably well. She wasn't crippled by anxiety. She had never spent an afternoon tucked in a fetal position on the floor (I only asked her because I certainly have). She took the kids to school, practiced law, did her shopping. From all outward appearances, she had the perfect life.

But something wasn't right. She couldn't sleep. Often she would lie awake all night long, her brain sizzling with worry. The sun would eventually rise. She would climb out of bed, furious at not having slept, and terrified about facing another day exhausted. *How would she make the kids' lunches? How would she wrangle a screaming toddler in the grocery store? How would she respond intelligently to a client in crisis?* Worry led to guilt. *I'm a bad wife, a bad mom, and a bad lawyer. How can I be good at anything if I'm always exhausted?!*

Guilt led to more worry. Anxiety began to boil. She was brave and made an appointment with her primary care physician. She also quietly saw a psychologist. Her doctor suggested medication. The psychologist suggested therapy. She wanted both, even recognized she needed both. And yet…she accepted neither.

"My family doesn't understand," she told me. "They tell me I just need to calm down, pray more, and trust Jesus." The tremor was now more pronounced. "But…it's just that…" She trailed off.

"You *do* trust Jesus?"

"Yes!" She said. "Yes. Exactly."

"But it's not helping."

She stayed quiet for a long time after that.

"It's okay," I said. "Jesus can handle your truth."

"What's wrong with me?"

She started crying in earnest now. That's when I told her about my nighttime. Without warning, I would awake to find my heart racing. Then a sting (was it real or imaginary?) would funnel down my arm. The very worst part came last. My brain would quietly tell me lies. *You're about to die. You're about to die. You're about to die. And there's nothing you can do about it.*

I would leap out of bed, nauseated and sweating, searching in vain for some relief. But there was no relief. When you're in the throes of a full-blown panic attack, nothing can be done for you, short of sedation. It's like being trapped on a turbulent airplane. There is nothing you can do but ride it out, telling yourself over and over that the plane isn't going to crash. You are not in the cockpit of your brain—control has been surrendered. I usually wound up on the floor, in the fetal position, scared out of my mind.

"So what did *you* do?" she asked me. "Did you see a therapist?"

"No. I did nothing. Not for a long time, anyway."

This is the saddest part. I chose the thing guaranteed to make my anxiety worse: *Hoping it goes away.* Why? Why didn't I seek out professional help when I so clearly needed it? I didn't seek help for the same reason my friend on the phone and millions of others do nothing when faced with a mental health challenge. We believe we've done all that can be done—we've prayed, gone to church, trusted God. And still we've suffered. Because of this, we wrongly assumed that there is something seriously wrong with our faith. We have done what our pastors and priests have told us to do. They said if we did these things, we would be delivered. But we haven't been.

So we suffer in silence and refuse the help we need because we believe we are beyond saving. *If I just increase my faith,* I thought, *this will all go away. I have the good news and power of Jesus. What else do I need?*

As it turns out, I needed quite a bit.

The good news of Jesus includes all the healing remedies we have at our disposal: community, doctors, therapy, and medication.

As Christians, we need first and foremost to turn to the church during times of trial and tribulation. There is nothing more powerfully healing than the love of God mediated through the church. Period. If I'm given only one option for help in a time of need, I'm choosing the church every time. Hands down. End. Of. Story.

Nevertheless, we can't forget that God also works outside of the church. God made the whole world and God loves and mediates love in and through the whole world. But we must have the eyes to see. Too often we stumble around in pain, silently begging God to help us without opening our eyes to see the helping hands that are readily available. This is particularly true when we face a mental health challenge. It's easier to be insular than vulnerable. We just want to close our eyes, snap our fingers, and have God fix it.

We're like the guy in the old joke who drowns in a flood. He's on his roof trying to escape the rising waters when he refuses a rescue boat and then a helicopter. When he gets to heaven, he wants to know why God didn't save him. God says, "What did you think the boat and helicopter were for?"

There are boats and helicopters all around us when it comes to mental health. We are fortunate in the United States; most areas have a plethora of mental health professionals.

In my experience, folks don't know where to start when they need a therapist. I'll tell you. Call your insurance company and ask for a list of providers. This is the fastest way to discover a professional near you who will also be affordable because he or she accepts your insurance.

That said, not all therapists are good therapists so I also suggest contacting a pastor at your church and asking for a list of therapists he or she trusts. Most churches keep this kind of list. Don't be embarrassed to ask for it. You're not the first, and I promise you won't be the last.

If you don't have a church or anyone you can trust to ask, then message me. Seriously. Email me. Facebook me. Call Church of the Incarnation in Dallas and ask to speak to me. I will help you. And if you are experiencing a genuine medical emergency, call 911.

Look, therapy—individual, couples, or group—has the potential to transform or even save your life. There are boats and helicopters circling your rising waters. There is no reason for you to go under.

I don't want to leave this topic without talking about the "M word:" medication. Some anxiety is so intense that medications are a must. There is nothing wrong with this. Depression and anxiety can be consequences of biology. If they are, healing often requires drugs. This is no different than having a cancer that requires chemotherapy to treat it. There is nothing inherently anti-Christian about using medication to treat mental health illness or disordered thinking. Let me say it again: Jesus is not mad that you need a pill to get out of bed in the morning. He does not see this as a lack of trust or love for him, a weakness or failure in your faith. He understands that you are fragile and wants you to have everything you need to feel strong. We are all fragile in some way. All of us need help. Nobody gets through this thing alone.

Unfortunately, our culture isn't quite as understanding as Jesus is, especially our church culture. There is still so much stigma attached to issues of mental health. We have a long way to go until we understand that anxiety and depression are just like diabetes and cancer. Some of us have to deal with them, others don't, and this has nothing to do with our character or spirituality. It's just who and how we are. We're humans. We're imperfect. That's okay. Feeling anxious or depressed does not mean our faith is damaged—not even when these emotions rise to the level of clinical diagnoses.

There is no judgment in the Christian community when a man goes to a cardiologist for a stress test because he's concerned about shortness of breath when climbing the stairs to his bedroom. But if that same man admitted his shortness of breath was caused by anxiety and not a blocked artery, judgment too often arrives. But why? Throughout Jesus' ministry, he heals both bodies and souls. The church must be willing to do the same. We have to proclaim loud and clear that the Gospel of Jesus Christ not only endorses doctors who care for the body, but also those who tend to the mind and soul as well.

When I finally broke down and saw a therapist for the first time, I told him I felt like a fraud. "I spend my life encouraging people to reach out and get the help they need. But..." I trailed off.

"You don't do it yourself?" he asked.

"Right."

"Right." He smiled. "But here you sit today."

My healing had begun.

I don't know if the woman who called me finally asked for help. But I think about her a lot, and I hope she knows that God takes no offense at her efforts to find healing. We must never forget that God is the Great Physician and desperately wants to heal our wounded souls.

If you are battling anxiety or depression, please know that this struggle does not mean your faith is weak. What it means is that you're dealing with something that roughly forty million Americans deal with every single day.

We *must* normalize this struggle. We *must* have this conversation. We *must* know we're not alone. When you wake up in the dead of night to find fear has infected your bones, certain no person has ever been this scared and you have no clue how you'll face tomorrow—remember that you are not alone.

I've been there. I know others who've been there, too. There are literally millions of us who have been there.

If you take nothing else from these words, please take this: You. Are. Not. Alone. And you never will be, ever.

But you need to reach out and ask for help. And for those of us who lead in the church, we must stand up and tell our people that if they are depressed, or anxious, or in marital distress, they should seek professional help and feel no shame in it.

Asking for help is never a sign of weakness, only strength.

And please remember, Jesus Christ has not come for the healthy. He has come for the sick. He has come for us.

clarence

Then they came to Capernaum; and when he was in the house he asked them, "What were you arguing about on the way?" But they were silent, for on the way they had argued with one another who was the greatest. He sat down, called the twelve, and said to them, "Whoever wants to be first must be last of all and servant of all." Then he took a little child and put it among them; and taking it in his arms, he said to them, "Whoever welcomes one such child in my name welcomes me, and whoever welcomes me welcomes not me but the one who sent me."

Mark 9:33-37

The phone rang early. Too early. The kind of early that lets you know immediately something is wrong.

"Hey, man," Colin said. "Ashley went into labor this morning. She had the baby."

"Oh," I said through the fog of morning brain. "That's great."

"No. It was too soon."

Of course, I thought. *It is too soon. Ashley's not due for several months.* "Oh," is what actually came out of my mouth. "What happened?"

"We lost him."

Colin and Ashley had recently moved back to Atlanta. They had been our next-door neighbors for several years, and we had grown close. Colin and I are opposites in just about every way. He played college football *and* rugby and now works in the construction industry. I played college theatre and held a hammer one time. But we became friends and spent more than a few evenings drinking beer and talking life in our respective yards. Then they headed back home to Atlanta to start a family.

Colin cleared his throat while I wiped the sleep out of my eyes. "So," he said, "the hospital wants to send in a chaplain, but we don't want some dude in here we don't know. I hate to put you on the spot, but can you talk to us? You can take a few minutes or whatever to gather your thoughts and call us back.

"Yes," I said. "Give me just a minute."

We hung up, and I looked out the window of our bedroom. Still dark out. I needed coffee.

Here's what you need to know. Colin and Ashley weren't going to church when we met. When they learned I was a pastor, they took pity on me and began showing up to our services to hear me preach. It was the most Southern, polite thing I've ever seen. I mean, they didn't go to church but they started going because their neighbor was a preacher. Who does that?

One evening Ashley surprised me. "Colin and I talk a lot about your sermons for the rest of our Sunday. It's strange how we keep coming back to different things you've said. We love it."

A seed of faith had been planted in their lives—it had nothing to do with me—God was at work. But we watered the seed with conversations in the backyard as the sun did its setting and the air its cooling. Those were good nights.

I hung up the phone and fell to my knees. "Jesus," I said. "I need you to come alongside me in the most tangible of ways. I need your words. I need your counsel. I need your presence. I need everything you've got. Give me whatever it is my friends need right now. Give me your peace, the one that passes all understanding, because I seriously have no idea what to say." Then I was out of time. The phone rang. Colin put me on speaker; Ashley spoke through her tears.

Their child lived for one hour. The doctor said the time the baby had was better spent in their arms than on an operating table. So that's what they did. Mom and Dad spent an hour holding their beloved boy before he died. They told me he looked exactly like Colin.

Out of respect for the sanctity of that moment, I'll leave the details of our conversation between us. It's enough to know that we prayed. We cried. We hung together as friends do when the world turns upside down and there's nothing to hold onto but each other. And Jesus showed up. He really showed up.

A few days later I flew to Atlanta to bury Clarence. That was the baby's name: Clarence.

He was a brave boy, that Clarence. Who among us has been asked to face death so quickly from the womb? Brave like his father, strong like his mother. If you've never seen a casket for an infant, you don't know this visual wound. There is something inherently wrong about burying a human so small. It's simply not how things are supposed to be. We are to live. Grow strong. And then those for whom we cared and grow strong watch over us as we become feeble and eventually die. That's the natural order of things. Parents aren't supposed to bury their children

Two summers ago, my older sister lost a child late in her pregnancy. Her labor had to be induced. All night she labored. When the sun rose, she gave birth to Benjamin whose soul had already taken flight. We put Benjamin's body in the ground and commended his spirit back to God. Under the heat of a Texas sun, I saw the deep pain in the eyes of my sister and her husband. It was a pain I had seen before in the eyes of Colin and Ashley.

There is no grief like that of losing a child—one need not experience the pain to know this—merely stand close to those who do. It will overwhelm you. It will suffocate you with the horror.

Why I am I writing about this? *Because this happens.* Because these babies lived. Because these babies died. And because so many of their parents suffer alone and in silence.

Miscarriages, stillbirths, and children who die within hours of birth happen far more often than any of us realize. And most people don't know what to do when these events happen. *Move on quickly and try to get pregnant again as soon as possible? Have a funeral and mourn for a year? Tell friends? Don't tell a soul?*

I don't know what the answer is, other than to say there's never one right way to handle tragedy, so don't let anyone tell you what you *must* do. It's your child who has died. *Your* child. But I pray you find some comfort in this: you share the child with another.

Children are never just our own; they are always God's because they come from God. I have heard people philosophize that we are formed in togetherness and born into separateness. I think this is what makes miscarriages so hard. The separateness never occurs. The child dies while still being very much together with the mother.

I don't know why infants die so early and so suddenly. Some people say it's God's will. Never believe them. It is not God's will to take unborn children from their parents. God doesn't want this to happen, and God doesn't cause this to happen. That would be unthinkable. We couldn't worship a God who did such things.

Here's what we know about what God actually does. God doesn't allow little ones to be alone. He surrounds them in love. If you've lost a little one, know this: your child is not alone. God has done with your baby what Jesus does in Mark's Gospel. God gathers the child in divine love, blesses the child, and sits the child down in the midst of the saints where he or she will be cared for for all of eternity.

We serve a God who teaches that our greatness lies in our willingness to welcome into our midst the weakest among us. We serve a God who loves and cares for the smallest and tiniest of people. No soul is ever overlooked, no person devalued because of the brevity of his or her life. God cares for your baby as much as any person God ever created.

I don't know where your baby is exactly in this moment. What I know is that God is infinitely good.

I pray that might be comfort for you.

fear

When it was evening on that day, the first day of the week, and the doors of the house where the disciples had met were locked for fear of the Jews, Jesus came and stood among them and said, "Peace be with you." After he said this, he showed them his hands and his side. Then the disciples rejoiced when they saw the Lord. Jesus said to them again, "Peace be with you. As the Father has sent me, so I send you." When he had said this, he breathed on them and said to them, "Receive the Holy Spirit. If you forgive the sins of any, they are forgiven them; if you retain the sins of any, they are retained."

John 20:19-23

I was in the bathroom at my parents' home when I realized I wasn't alone. A squirrel had joined me so I retreated into the shower to put some distance between this monster and me. You may be thinking, *What's the big deal? It's a squirrel.* But squirrels frighten me. They're like rats, only bigger and faster and meaner. And *clearly* smarter. I mean, how did the squirrel even get into the bathroom? We'll never know.

The door to the bathroom was shut, and the squirrel was going totally nuts, running in a crazed loop, careening off the walls. It was madness, and it was only a matter of time until the squirrel came for me. And when it came for me, I knew it would not be good.

I took a deep breath and assessed the situation. Door closed. No cell phone in my pocket. No one else home in the house. I had two options: Wait to be rescued and pray the squirrel didn't eat me, or make a run for it.

I wish I could say I made this decision quickly. I didn't. It took some time to summon the courage to face the super rodent. But I got there. Eventually.

I took a deep breath and ran—screaming the entire time. The squirrel banged against my body, got tangled in my legs, and was just about to put my head in its mouth when I reached the door and flung it open. The squirrel and I burst out of the bathroom. I sprinted outside, and the squirrel ran off to some new place in the house.

From the safety of my car in the driveway, I called for backup. The squirrel was eventually captured hours later, with the help of a far braver man.

Fear is a powerful thing, isn't it? It doesn't matter if you're scared of a tiny little squirrel or a hungry leopard. If you're scared, then you are scared.

I have been scared many times in my life—and not just by squirrels. When I moved to a city where I didn't have a single friend, I was scared. I spent long nights alone, watching other people go to dinner or walk hand-in-hand, fearing I would never find a friend.

One time, I was taking a law exam and had no idea what the test was asking. I left the classroom and hid in the bathroom for nearly half an hour. I almost didn't return to class. Another time, existential fear gripped my soul when I could no longer believe God actually cared about my life. I mean, children were starving in Africa and being crucified in Iraq by religious extremists. Did God *really* care whether or not I could pay back my student loan? The whole notion that I mattered at all to God became crazy to me. That was about as scary a thought as I've ever had. A close second was when my wife and I were first married. We had no money and were facing an unexpected, very large debt that needed to be paid.

You know these fears. We all have our personal versions of them. Fear is an utterly universal human experience. I was on a plane once when the captain told us we had blown a tire on takeoff, and our landing would be of the emergency variety. I looked around the cabin at total strangers and knew exactly what they were feeling. I saw it in their eyes. I'm sure they saw it mine. We were afraid—every last one of us.

In life, there is no escaping fear. There is only what we do with it.

Pentecost is the day God pours his Holy Spirit onto and into the church. The disciples are gathered and the Spirit of God comes upon them in such a way that people from many different countries speaking many different languages can suddenly understand one another. The Holy Spirit unifies diversity in a miraculous way, and the church grows by thousands. Pentecost is a neat story—and it's a story I believe. But if I'm honest, it's not a story that I can relate to because I have never experienced anything like it. In the passage from John's Gospel, we hear a less familiar Pentecost story. For John, Pentecost occurs in a place of fear, and that's something that resonates in my soul.

John says it's evening and the disciples are huddled together in a house. The doors of the house are closed—and not just closed, but locked because the disciples are afraid. Jesus has been crucified. Everything they believe is now up for grabs. Frightened, they must have wondered, *Are we next?* And so they sit in fear, trembling in anticipation of a knock at a door they do not want to open.

Do you have doors like that—doors you know you ought to open but are afraid to? I know I do. It's the dirt we sweep under the rug, the bill we immediately throw in the trash because we can't stomach opening the envelope to see what's inside, the doctor's appointment that we should have made two years ago, the call you don't want to make because you know you were wrong, but you're not ready to admit it.

What are the doors you don't want to open?

It's hard for me to imagine the disciples being afraid. After all, they have witnessed Jesus' power firsthand. They know, better than anyone, that he is in control. But when he dies and they can no longer see him, they are filled with fear and doubt.

We struggle to believe in that which we cannot see—especially in today's culture where we demand evidence for everything. If an event isn't captured on YouTube or Instagram, it's (almost) as if it never happened. But the Bible says that "faith is the assurance of things hoped for, the conviction of things not seen" (Hebrews 11:1). I'm all for evidence, but some truths simply can't be seen in the ways our modern culture likes. Not all truth can be proven, but that doesn't make it any less true. I love my wife and children more than my own life, but I can't prove this. I can live my life in a manner that reflects this truth, but it can't be empirically proven in a laboratory. Likewise, I believe it's true that to forgive is better than holding a grudge. I imagine most people believe this to be true, but none of us can actually *prove* it. Some truths simply cannot be proven.

We face this conundrum with the truth that Jesus Christ was raised from the dead. This is the truth the disciples are being asked to believe before Pentecost. Jesus has been killed and his body is in a tomb. There are whispers that he has risen but that is hard to believe, especially when the disciples are sitting behind closed and locked doors, fearing they will be next upon the cross.

Fear, if we let it, will keep us imprisoned behind the locked doors of our lives. And that is no place for a follower of Jesus. God calls us into the world to do hard work, work that will be scary sometimes. I can't think of a single character in the Bible God called to a safe mission. Abraham? Moses? Jacob? Joseph? Esther? King David? Rahab? Remind me who God asks to go to the Bahamas and sip piña coladas?

Not. A. One. God is good, and God's Spirit will always lead to goodness, but there is no promise that this goodness will be safe.

Here's the deal: I can guarantee you almost nothing about what will happen to you if you follow God's Spirit. But I know one thing for certain: Your life will be good because God will you use you to bless the world. You won't just be good—you will be good for something.[1]

Jesus breathes on his disciples and says, *Go and forgive the sins of the people. As my Father has sent me, so I send you.* There is nothing safe about the mission God sends Jesus to accomplish. Why should we think it will be any different for us?

Besides, what's the alternative? Draw the shades, lock the doors, and sit tight? I want to do that some days. Like the disciples, I want

---

1   Philosopher Henry David Thoreau said, "Be not simply good—be good for something." It's a great line, but he stole it from Jesus.

to crawl into a safe space with the door locked and stay perfectly still. But I can't. Every time I lock myself in, I lock someone else out. And it's not Jesus. Locked doors don't work on him. But they work on everyone else, and these people might be afraid too and in need of the spirit of God in their lives, a spirit that I might be called to share. Jesus does not give us his spirit so we can cower behind locked doors. He gives it so we might share it with others.

Imagine if the disciples stay in the house. What if they never open that door? Never take the Holy Spirit outside? I'm sure they are still scared even after Jesus breathes his Spirit upon them. A transcendent experience with God fires you up for a time, but emotion fades. The disciples still face a great deal of uncertainty beyond that door. But they open it anyway.

Why? How? The disciples realize that whatever they will need on the outside has already come inside. They have been given the Spirit of God. Somehow they garner the courage to trust that this is enough.

Whatever is waiting for you, whatever lurks on the other side of your door, know this: *You have what you need. You are not alone.* The Spirit of God has been poured out in power and it is with you. I don't know how things will go, but I know how you will go—with God.

There is no escaping fear—only what we do with it. M. Scott Peck was a doctor whose writing I greatly admire. As a teenager, he came home from Philips Exeter Academy for spring vacation and told his parents he wasn't going back. His parents couldn't understand why he wasn't happy—Exeter was the best education money could buy. Peck couldn't articulate why, either, only that the thought of returning was unbearable to him. His parents took him to a psychiatrist who diagnosed him as clinically depressed and suggested a one-month hospitalization.

Peck went home that night to think about his options. He said this was the only night of his life he considered suicide. Returning to school was the safe, secure, and productive path for his life. Not returning was unsafe, unknown, unpredictable. But he knew what he had to do. The next morning he went to the psychiatrist and told him he would never return to Exeter, but he was ready to walk through the door of the hospital.

A lot of people think our culture is built on the fear of death, but I heard a minister say something recently that caught my ear. He said our culture isn't based on fear of death but rather on the fear of being raised from the dead. I think he's right. To allow the Spirit to lead us, change us, transform us, is frightening.

Change is scary—it always was and always will be. Spiritual growth requires courage. When Peck grew up, he became a psychiatrist and said: "Courage is not the absence of fear; it is the making of action in spite of fear, the moving out against the resistance engendered by fear into the unknown and into the future."

There are doors in our lives that we need to open. Doors Jesus wants us to walk through—doors to our future and doors to our change.

Change is scary. I know you're scared, and I am too. Don't forget: Jesus knows we are scared. After his resurrection, when he appears at the tomb to Mary, the first thing he tells her is that she doesn't need to be afraid.

In life, there is no escaping fear; there's only deciding what we do with it. What will you do with fear today? Will you allow it to keep you locked inside or will you acknowledge that the Spirt of God has joined you in the darkened room?

Don't you want to know what's on the other side of your closed door?

Come on. Open the door. You can push it slowly; you can peek out before you venture out. But open the door. And when you're ready, walk right through it, trusting that whatever you need *out there* has already come *in here*.

only the servants knew

On the third day there was a wedding in Cana of Galilee, and the mother of Jesus was there. Jesus and his disciples had also been invited to the wedding. When the wine gave out, the mother of Jesus said to him, "They have no wine." And Jesus said to her, "Woman, what concern is that to you and to me? My hour has not yet come." His mother said to the servants, "Do whatever he tells you." Now standing there were six stone water jars for the Jewish rites of purification, each holding twenty or thirty gallons. Jesus said to them, "Fill the jars with water." And they filled them up to the brim. He said to them, "Now draw some out, and take it to the chief steward." So they took it. When the steward tasted the water that had become wine, and did not know where it came from (though the servants who had drawn the water knew), the steward called the bridegroom and said to him, "Everyone serves the good wine first, and then the inferior wine after the guests have become drunk. But you have kept the good wine until now." Jesus did this, the first of his signs, in Cana of Galilee, and revealed his glory; and his disciples believed in him.

John 2:1-11

I got into a verbal altercation about an hour into my time at seminary. Actually, seminary had not even started yet—this was orientation. I was at a round table doing an icebreaker exercise when the conversation turned theological. The question that arose was this: What does it mean to be a disciple of Jesus?

Some very good and intellectually complicated (if not bloated) answers were given. Lots of fancy theological words were used as folks tried to impress each other with how much they knew about the Bible, history, and most of all, Jesus. Now, these were good, smart people, some of whom became my friends. But I became highly annoyed. Christians can be really frustrating—especially those trying to become *professional* Christians.

The truth of the matter is that I've never thought following Jesus is hard to understand. The actual doing of it? Yes. Following Jesus is extraordinarily hard, and I fail more than I succeed. But the definition of what it means to follow Jesus? That's not hard. It's simple. We complicate it because we want to avoid it.

So in my annoyance I said, "Well, the point is to love God, right?"

The table nodded.

"Then it's easy," I said. "Jesus tells us exactly what we will do if we love him." I even quoted scripture like a real moron. "John 14:23. Anyone who loves me will obey my teaching. Verse 24: Anyone who does not love me will not obey my teaching. These words you hear are not my own; they belong to the Father who sent me."

The entire table rolled their eyes, and the argument heated up. I was making it too simple, they said. I was being legalistic, they said. I was being naïve.

And maybe I was? After all…I'm all those things: simple, legalistic, naïve. But in this case, I was also something else. I was right.

If discipleship doesn't involve obedience, why does Jesus waste so much time telling us how we ought to live? He could have performed a bunch of miracles, died on a cross, and then risen to glorious life. Mission accomplished. Finished. Done!

But that's not what he does. Jesus gives us commands. He shows us how to live—how to *really* live.

Consider the passage that starts this essay: It's familiar to many. Jesus goes to a wedding and turns water to wine. Running out of wine would have been a massive embarrassment for the host. So Mary the Mother of God nudges her son and basically says, *Yo, kid, do one of your tricks.*

Woman, he says. *Shh! It's not my time.*

Mary gives him the stink eye. *You better do as I say...*

Jesus gets up from the table—he knows who is in charge. (I love imagining all the times Mary bosses him around. Think about it. She *knows* who Jesus is. She knows *why* he has come into the world. Like any good mother, she wants her son to be the man he is born to be.) So Mary looks at the servants and says, *Do whatever my son tells you to do.*

This is where it gets really good. Jesus says to the servants, "Fill the jars with water." They obey.

Then he says, "Now draw some out, and take it to the chief steward." They obey. John reports that when the steward tastes the water, it had become wine. But he doesn't know where it has come from. So the steward says to the bridegroom, *Everyone serves the good stuff first and the cheap stuff after the guests are drunk. But you've kept the good wine until now.*

And with that, glasses are raised, toasts are made, and the party rolls on.

It's a terrific story, but what does it have to do with obedience and discipleship? Everything—it has everything to do with discipleship.

Some people see this story as nothing more than a glorified beer run. Keg runs dry; Jesus refills it. What a totally cool guy. This interpretation misses an important point. Do you notice? *Only the servants know what happened.*

The steward doesn't know. The guests don't know. The bridegroom doesn't know. The only people who know the water has been turned to wine are the servants who obey Jesus.

"Fill the jars with water," he says.

Yes, sir, they say. They see the miracle, and *only* they see the miracle.

So. What does it mean to be a disciple of Jesus? Doing what Jesus says to do. It's in following and obeying that we witness the work of God. It's there, in chasing after Jesus, that we see miracles.

Obedience isn't about blind allegiance or legalism. It's about following a man who turns water to wine, a man who knows how to live life to the fullest. And trusting that following his commands will also reveal this to you. There is no adventure like discipleship. None.

At his fiftieth birthday concert, the late David Bowie said, "I don't know where I'm going from here, but I promise it won't be boring." The same can be said of all disciples. It's not drudgery—it's the most exciting thing you could ever do. To see God, to experience God, to become like God. Drugs won't do that. Money won't do that. Sex won't do that.

John Barclay, the late Scottish minister and author, points out that every story in the Gospel of John tells not of something Jesus does once but of something Jesus is forever doing. I would take it a step further and say the gospel tells us not only of something Jesus does once but also that he is forever doing *through us in our obedience to God.*

Near the end of Matthew's Gospel, Jesus tells his followers what the final judgment of God will look like. It's an incredible scene. Jesus will sit on his throne and all the nations of the world will gather before him to be judged. But the standard by which they will be judged is a surprising one. There is no Bible memory test, theological quiz, or question about church attendance. Instead, Jesus says, "Come, you that are blessed by my Father, inherit the kingdom prepared for you from the foundation of the world; for I was hungry and you gave me food, I was thirsty and you gave me something to drink, I was a stranger and you welcomed me, I was naked and you gave me clothing, I was sick and you took care of me, I was in prison and you visited me." Those who hear these words of Jesus are confused. "Lord," they say, "when was it that we saw you hungry and gave you food, or thirsty and gave you something to drink? And when was it that we saw you a stranger and welcomed you, or naked and gave you clothing? And when was it that we saw you sick or in prison and visited you?"

Jesus replies back: *Whenever you did this for the least of these, you did it to me.*

Let this sit with you for a moment. Jesus will judge our lives by our willingness (or unwillingness) to continue his work in this world. What matters most to God is not what we know but whether or not we obey Jesus by blessing people in the same ways he does. The good news of Jesus Christ is that God has given us the privilege and responsibility of making Christ continually present in this world.

The good news of Jesus Christ isn't just that he has done stuff in ancient Palestine but that he is still acting today—in Dallas and Los Angeles and Hong Kong and in every city and village and farm around the world.

Recently, I experienced the reality of this good news when I was driving on a crowded street in Dallas. I was stopped in traffic—again—when I saw in my rearview mirror the car behind me making no effort to stop before coming into contact with my car. I braced for impact. Fortunately, the collision wasn't too bad—no injuries—but there was the cringeworthy crunch of car-on-car action. I flipped on my emergency flashers, pulled into an adjacent parking lot, and rolled down my window to motion for the other driver to follow me. And that's when it happened—the other driver and I made eye contact. She saw my clerical collar, and while I can't know what she was thinking, I assume it was something like this: *SO LONG, SUCKER.* Because that's when she floored it. Like that, she was gone. My immediate reaction was to throw my car into reverse and chase her down. Anger consumed me. I couldn't believe I had just been involved in a hit-and-run! I was really, really mad.

Then I had another thought: *Ryan,* I asked myself, *What are you going to do? Get into a high-speed chase wearing a clerical collar? Force this woman off the road and make a citizen's arrest?* I shifted my car into park and let out a long sigh.

No, I thought. *I'm not going to do that. Instead, I'm going to do something completely different. I am going to be grateful nobody was hurt, and then I'm going to LET. IT. GO.*

I didn't want to let it go, but I figured Jesus probably wanted me to. He tells us "You have heard that it was said, 'You shall love your neighbor and hate your enemy.' But I say to you, Love your enemies and pray for those who persecute you, so that you may be children of your Father in heaven; for he makes his sun rise on the evil and on the good, and sends rain on the righteous and on the unrighteous. For if you love those who love you, what reward do you have? Do not even the tax collectors do the same?" (Matthew 5:43-46).

As soon as I made the decision to let it go, relief washed over me, and the anger slid instantly out of my heart. I don't always obey Jesus, but when I do, I give myself the opportunity to experience what the servants in Cana experience: a miracle. You can too.

There is a danger here, however, that must be addressed. Taking obedience to Jesus seriously can be dangerous because we are fallible human beings who will not do it perfectly. Giving food to the hungry and drink to thirsty and clothing to the naked sounds good in theory. Who doesn't want to do these things?

Me. That's who. Just not all the time.

That's okay. Nobody is going to obey Jesus every moment of their entire lives. This is where grace comes into the picture. Jesus calls us to carry on his work but understands that we can't—or won't—some of the time.

When I serve at the altar on Sundays, a single thought runs through my head. Do you want to know what it is?

It's this: *I'm so unworthy. I'm so unworthy. I'm so unworthy, because I'm so disobedient. I have unclean lips. I have selfish desires. I have a prideful spirit. I am so unworthy.*

I think this. And then do you know what I do? I carry on serving at the altar—not because I deserve to but because God loves me in spite of my unworthiness. On my own, I am not worthy. None of us are. Jesus' love makes me worthy and able to stand before God and my community.

In my church when we confess our sins, we ask forgiveness for "things done and things left undone." When we pray these words, I imagine most people think primarily about "things done" and then feel guilty about them. That is okay—sometimes we need to feel guilty. Sometimes we do bad things, and we need to repent.

But for a moment, cut yourself some slack for the "things done" in your life and meditate on the "things undone." Meditate on what Jesus is calling you to do. Meditate on the areas of your life where Jesus is asking for your obedience. What holds you back?

I have two sons—three years old and 18 months. Neither of them obeys me very often. But do you know what they both do? They love me. I know this in spite of their disobedience. I know they love me because I'm their father, and fathers know the hearts of their children—even when their hearts cannot be seen in their actions.

Your Heavenly Father knows that you love him even when you disobey. When we don't do what our God asks, we withhold our love for him, withholding from a God who loved us enough to climb up on the hard wood of a cross.

In disobedience, we miss out. Imagine if one of the servants had chosen not to obey Mary. Instead of following Jesus to fill the jugs with water, imagine he goes out to smoke a cigarette instead. He would have missed the miracle. He would have missed Jesus.

Jesus may be asking you to do something you don't want to do, something you think is pointless, or hard, or boring. But you don't know what you might get to see unless you do this thing.

Go and pour the water into the jug, Jesus says. What on earth could be more mundane? Then again, we might see water turned to wine.

god
of the
dark

"But in those days, after that suffering, the sun will be darkened, and the moon will not give its light, and the stars will be falling from heaven, and the powers in the heavens will be shaken. Then they will see 'the Son of Man coming in clouds' with great power and glory.

Mark 13:24-26

May I ask you a question? Nobody else is listening. It's just you and me. Ready? Okay, here it is.

What are you afraid of? We're all afraid of something. Illness? Retirement? Advanced math? Loneliness? What is it for you?

We all share certain existential fears—death, loneliness, a meaningless life. Some fears are universal, but many of them aren't. Talk to ten different people about fear and you'll hear ten different stories. It could be snakes (or squirrels!), tall buildings, or routine visits to the dentist. Just thinking about that little drill raises my blood pressure. We're all wired differently, which means our fears are too.

Some fears are healthy. There's a reason we move cautiously at the edge of a cliff—death is one wrong step away. Other fears however, aren't so healthy. Consider the fear that keeps us from apologizing to someone we've harmed. We may want to apologize, but the word "Sorry" is scary. Some fears keep us alive, and other fears keep us from living.

Fear: It's complicated. This should totally be on a bumper sticker.

When I was a kid I had a particularly ferocious fear. I was afraid of small spaces—hopelessly claustrophobic. On more than one occasion, my poor mother had to reassure strangers that no, she wasn't kidnapping me. It was simply necessary to drag her child onto the department store elevator. Oh, how I hated those tiny chambers of death! Small spaces—dark rooms with no escape— filled in the contours of my nightmares.

Years ago I fainted in the middle of the night and awoke on my bathroom floor in total darkness. I couldn't see, and for a moment, I couldn't move. My body was wedged between the door to my bathroom and the cabinet beneath my sink. I honestly thought I had been buried alive—my worst nightmare come true.

Once I managed to find my feet, I grabbed my cell phone and called my wife (we were still dating then). I said, "Get over here! I don't know what happened, but I'm pretty certain I'm dying!"

She drove over, took care of me, and told me to *stop being dramatic.* She tells me this about once a week. But hey, darkness can be scary. And it doesn't matter if you're seven or twenty-seven.

Ask Jamie Foxx. When Foxx played Ray Charles in the blockbuster movie, *Ray,* the director asked if Foxx would be willing to have his eyes sealed shut while filming. Desperate to give the best performance of his life, Foxx agreed. For up to fourteen hours a day,

Foxx wore specially created prosthetics that took away his sight. Foxx said it was like being buried alive—he suffered terrible spells of hyperventilation trying to cope with the inescapable darkness. Before he could get down to the business of acting, Foxx had to first overcome the crippling anxiety of being unable to escape the dark.

Isn't that how many of us feel about the darkness in our lives? We simply want to escape it, but in our lesson for this essay, Jesus suggests we do something else with darkness. Notice it, and then, be comforted by it.

In the passage Jesus is talking about his second coming, telling the disciples what it will look and feel like in the days just before he returns. Christians believe that Jesus will return from heaven and restore all of creation to originally intended perfection. But in "those days," Jesus says, "the sun will be darkened, and the moon will not give its light; the stars will fall from heaven, and the powers of heaven will be shaken. Then the sign of the Son of Man will appear in heaven."

I was raised in a Christian tradition that routinely associated the second coming of Jesus with catastrophic earthly events. The basic thrust of the message was that the world would someday fall apart— but when it did, Jesus would return to rescue Christians from the destruction. It was a dreary picture of the future.

This forecast never made much sense to me. What was the point of God creating anything if it was *always* going to end badly? I could never make sense of that in my head. Surely what began with a cosmic burst of glorious light in Genesis wasn't going to go up in flames in Revelation, right? But this is what I was taught. Because of this teaching, I feared the second coming. A lot. The whole thing sounded terrifying. So much so that I didn't want Jesus to come back—not even if he *was* going to save me. I didn't want the world to plunge into chaos and darkness. I wanted the light of Jesus to spread and spread and spread, and I didn't want this light to only spread after all the Christians were safely swept back up to heaven. I want it now, while everyone on earth still has a chance to bask in the warmth of divine light.

I still haven't figured what will happen when Jesus returns. Despite claims to the contrary, no one else knows either. I simply believe that Jesus will return—and when he does, it's going to be great because that is what God always intended.

None of this changes the fact that Jesus himself says dark days will happen. What does he mean by this? I've spent years trying to answer this question. I've read books, listened to sermons, and asked countless Christians what they think. After all that study, this is the conclusion I've come to: It doesn't matter.

What matters is that Jesus wants us to know that when we face our darkest days, when the sun and moon can no longer be counted on for light, God still can be. *The whole earth may crumble,* Jesus says, *but I never will.*

One of the people I love most in this world has recently had a few difficult years. Just before Christmas of last year, she came to me and said, "I want to pull the covers over my head and wake up on December 26."

"Yeah," I said. "I know that feeling."

I believe Jesus knows that feeling too. This is why he reminds us over and over again that light will come eventually. But since we don't know when, we must wait, and we must watch. We must be like servants tending our masters' house while they are away. They might come home at any moment—evening, midnight, dawn—

who knows? Nobody does. So we wait, and we watch. And there will be surely days when we pull the covers over our heads.

But here's what we don't do. Here's what we *can't* do—we can't stop believing. hoping. and watching for the light. We cannot allow the darkness of cynicism—so pervasive these days—to take hold of our hearts and minds.

This is not easy, not when we see unarmed black men gunned down by white police officers. widespread corruption in government, when terrorists massacre innocent civilians, when we lose our jobs or our spouses walk out on us.

If I'm honest, sometimes I fear the darkness will never end. But then I remember what Jesus says about the sky falling and the heavens shaking and how then—in a moment of utter darkness—he will return to us.

Yes, it's dark, and it's easy to believe we will be let down in the end, that there's nothing worth waiting for. But Jesus says: *Hold on. Wait. Watch. I am coming, and I am worth the wait.*

I don't know what lurks in your darkness. But I know something about it—it's scary. I also know it might not go away anytime soon. But I also know something else—God may be light but he comes in the dark. There is no dark water God won't wade into; no dark night he won't spend at our side. We may be afraid of the dark, but God isn't. He made the dark and in it, he moves.

In her wonderful book, *Learning to Walk in the Dark,* Barbara Brown Taylor counts about a hundred references to darkness in the Bible. And most of them are bad. Sinners are cast into darkness, plagues darken the sun, and we're told that if our eye is evil, our whole body will be full of darkness. But if you look closer, Brown Taylor says you can find another side to darkness.

God tells Abraham to look up to the stars and try to count them, if he wants to know how many descendants he'll have. His grandson Jacob wrestles all night with God and comes away with a new name: Israel. Then Jacob's son Joseph starts interpreting dreams, which come at night, and this is the skill that ends up saving him when he is betrayed by his brothers. A bit later, Moses leads God's people out of bondage and across the Red Sea. When? At night. This is also when manna falls to keep them alive as they wander toward the Promised Land. Fast forward to Bethlehem and a teenage girl gives birth to a baby boy in a barn in the dead of night. Jump ahead thirty years and see that same boy, now a man, dead in a dark tomb. In the morning, he is gone. His resurrection, the singular moment of glory, happens at night, in the suffocating darkness of a cave.

God is light, but God's best work is done in the dark.

As a teenager, I was still frightened of small, dark places. But my dad decided we were going to learn to scuba dive. If there's one thing a claustrophobic kid wants to avoid at all costs, it's breathing air out of a tiny hose a hundred feet under water.

But we did it. To pass the course we had to dive in a cold lake with visibility often limited to just a few inches. This was not easy for me. Near the end of the dive, our instructor led us to a tunnel. It was pitch black, and I couldn't see where it ended.

But I knew what I had to do. I swam toward it and entered the darkness. And I kicked like crazy until I came out the other side. My dad has always praised my courage on this day. He was so proud of the way I confidently swam into that tunnel. But I'll tell you the truth: I was scared out of my mind. The only reason I swam into that tunnel of death was because my father was behind me. I knew that whatever happened, I wouldn't be alone. I couldn't see my dad, but I felt his presence. He was with me, and I knew he would be there until we reached the other side.

Jesus will return some day. He will bring light to brighten our darkened world. But until then, may we trust that our Father in heaven does not wait to meet us in the light, but walks (and swims) with us now—this day—in our dark.

it's never over

When the sabbath was over, Mary Magdalene, and Mary the mother of James, and Salome bought spices, so that they might go and anoint him. And very early on the first day of the week, when the sun had risen, they went to the tomb. They had been saying to one another, "Who will roll away the stone for us from the entrance to the tomb?" When they looked up, they saw that the stone, which was very large, had already been rolled back. As they entered the tomb, they saw a young man, dressed in a white robe, sitting on the right side; and they were alarmed. But he said to them, "Do not be alarmed; you are looking for Jesus of Nazareth, who was crucified. He has been raised; he is not here. Look, there is the place they laid him. But go, tell his disciples and Peter that he is going ahead of you to Galilee; there you will see him, just as he told you." So they went out and fled from the tomb, for terror and amazement had seized them; and they said nothing to anyone, for they were afraid.

Mark 16:1-8

It all begins and ends with Easter.

So let's end our time together there too.

"You are looking for Jesus."

These are the words of an angel. He is dressed in white and standing in the place where Jesus' body is supposed to be.

"He is not here." The angel is talking to Mary Magdalene. She doesn't reply. How can she? *He is not here.* What a thing for a person to say! Especially a person standing by the tomb where the body of your best friend is supposed to be.

Jesus has risen from the dead. That's what we say on Easter. It's why Christians gather in sacred places of worship from Brooklyn to Cairo. It's why we have celebrated Easter for more than twenty centuries. Jesus has risen from the dead. That's what we say.

This is totally insane. And totally true.

All living things die. We pick up on this fact as children. We see dead leaves on the ground while being pulled in our little red wagons. We go for a car ride and notice some poor dog lying on the side of the road, his rib cage perfectly still. Something tells us he isn't napping. Long before we can ever think to articulate what death means, we know the truth. All that lives will die.

The poet T.S. Eliot wrote,
> *I have seen the moment of my greatness flicker,*
> *And I have seen the eternal Footman hold my coat*
> *   and snicker,*
> *And I am afraid.*

That's how I feel. Afraid. Jesus has risen from the dead? How can we believe this when logic dictates that we should not? How can this impossible claim be true?

This is a theological sticking point for a lot of people. No matter how many times they hear the story, they can't arrive at a place of declaring that a dead man was resurrected.

But Christians do. And for centuries, Christians have proclaimed that Christ has risen from the dead. And we have not just said it with our mouths but we have believed it in our hearts, and our lives have and been transformed by this truth.

A friend traveled high with a small team into the Himalayas. The people they met had never heard the name of Jesus, but they were deeply religious.

The mountain folks worshiped an angry god who required them to do awful things, things they didn't want to do but felt they had to. This group still practiced child sacrifice, believing their god required the most valuable sacrifices they could offer. Once a generation, one of the families offered a child as sacrifice. The burden would then pass to another family in the next generation.

Sometimes people tell me that beliefs don't matter. "Believe whatever you want," they say. "Everyone is entitled to believe in anything or everything." While we may debate the veracity of this statement, the more important issue is honesty about the effects of beliefs. Because those people living in the mountains of Nepal believed their god was angry, a child was murdered every generation. Sure, this is an extreme example, but in my own life I've known people imprisoned by belief. I have sat with them, looked into their eyes, and seen the shackles around their hearts and their minds—the woman who won't leave an abusive husband, the teenager who thinks he's worthless because somebody said so.

Beliefs matter. In fact, your beliefs—perhaps more than anything else—will shape the course of your life.

What do you believe?

My friend told the Himalayan villagers about the God of the Bible and how God had given up his own son to save the world. He told them a perfect sacrifice had been made, which meant all the other sacrifices could stop. Do you know what they said? "We always hoped something like this could be true." *We always hoped.*

On that first Easter morning, hope is in short supply. Jesus is dead, and the disciples are scattered. For three years, they have followed a teacher unlike any the world has ever seen.

This teacher says, *Ask and it will be given; seek, and you shall find; knock, and the door will be opened for you.* He is a holy man who has spent his days and nights with folks who are considered anything but holy. He stands up to bullies. When the religious leaders try to stone a woman for adultery, he says, *Okay, but do me a favor. Let the one of you who hasn't sinned throw the first stone.* Nobody is stoned that day.

Jesus is a man like no other. But then he dies and becomes just like every other man. So the disciples split town. Jesus has promised so much—salvation, mercy, grace, new life. He tells them that if the temple is destroyed, he can rebuild it in three days.

Then their teacher, their friend, is arrested, beaten, and hung upon a cross. So the disciples leave. It's easy to criticize the disciples because we know the rest of the story. But imagine being there. Imagine having your every hope destroyed.

Last year, I listened to a man speak on behalf of some families who lost children in a terrible plane crash in the Alps. The pilot of the plane intentionally crashed, killing everyone on board. Can you imagine?

With a quiver in his voice, the man tried to describe what the parents have experienced. But there aren't really words. To raise a child until she's a sophomore in high school and then to lose her like *that.* There are no words.

That's what profound loss does to us. We don't know what to say, we don't know what to do, and we don't know what to believe.

Jesus' death is profound for the disciples. On the very night that Jesus is arrested, Peter tells his friend: *I will never leave you. These others might but not me.* But of course Peter does. At the first opportunity, he turns his back on Jesus. He doesn't know Jesus. He's never even met the man.

I'll be honest. I sympathize with Peter because Peter *wants* to believe. He is the first out of the boat to follow Jesus, the first to pull a sword to defend Jesus, and the first to publicly disown him. Peter is, like so many of us, conflicted about who Jesus is. He wants to believe, but he isn't sure he wants to die. Peter is scared. Just like me.

Are you scared?

Not everyone in the story is scared, though. Mary Magdalene stands at the cross while Jesus dies. She doesn't stop there or run away. She comes to the tomb; she knows Jesus is dead. She is not expecting a miracle; she's worried about moving the stone because she wants to anoint the body of her friend. She has loved Jesus in life, and she wants to love him in death.

But the stone has been rolled away. Jesus is gone.

Do not be afraid, the angel says. *You're looking for Jesus. He has risen. He is not here. But go, tell his disciples and Peter that he is going before you to Galilee; there you will see him.*

And then Mary Magdalene does what most of us would do. She runs like hell—and she doesn't say anything to anyone, not at first. Stand at the cross? *No problem.* Go to the tomb? *No problem.* Obey the scary angel in the garden? *No thank you.*

But again, we know the story. Mary Magdalene eventually tells Peter everything. What changes for her? How does she move from fear to belief? The only way anyone does—they meet the Risen Lord.

Mary experiences Jesus after his death, and she knows that what she thinks is the end is just the beginning. So she goes to Peter and tells him the good news: the one they trusted with their lives is worthy of it.

Ever since then, Christians have called Christ's death a substitute, a sacrifice, a ransom. What matters most—I think—is that we call it a victory. The Bible says Jesus tastes death for everyone—and through death, renders death powerless. It's true that all who live must die. It is also true that all who die can live again because there is no force on earth or in hell that can defeat the power of God.

That doesn't mean this life will be easy. I heard a preacher on TV say, "If you pray to God, then everything that's wrong in your life is about to get good." And I thought, *How dare you?*

There are cancers that will not go into remission. There are accidents that will befall us. There are marriages that will crumble. There are parents in Germany and Kenya and Newtown and Ferguson who no longer hold their babies.

I have watched as my own family members have suffered in ways I could never have imagined. God doesn't protect us from suffering and death. God does something better. He suffers and dies with us so we might rise again. God lets us die and brings us back to life.

Do you need to be brought back to life today?

Consider Jesus' message to Mary. What does he want her to know? First: He's alive. And second: the one who betrayed him, Peter, needs to know this news.

Go tell Peter, he says. *Go tell Peter. I want him to come to Galilee—not to be condemned but forgiven. I want to give him a second chance.*

I don't know what you've been through. I don't know your pain or your sin. What I know is that whatever it is, you can bring it to Jesus. Peter disowns Jesus. And Peter is one of the first people Jesus wants to talk to.

Jesus wants to talk to you, too.

An old girlfriend of mine once told me, "I don't like it when Christians talk about being forgiven by God."

"Why not?" I asked.

"Because it's like saying you can live however you want and then get born again, or whatever, and then the past doesn't matter. Sounds like b.s."

"I hear you," I said. "But that's not really what we believe. It's not that the past doesn't matter. It's that the past matters too much. I can't take back my words. I can't heal my wounds. I can't forgive my sin." I took a deep breath. "All I can do is accept the mercy of God and then offer it to others."

Being a Christian doesn't erase our pasts. It assures us that God accepts us in spite of them. Maybe we believe that. Maybe we don't. But let me ask you something: If you don't believe this, do you wish you did?

Is there any part of your heart that's like the hearts of the people in Nepal, hoping Jesus is true? If there is, do me a favor. Follow Peter to Galilee. Imagine how scared he must be. Feel his shame. Imagine how hard it is to face Jesus.

And then see the moment he sees Jesus, smiling, loving, forgiving. And then watch as Peter rises from death to life.

A friend to sinners.

A victor over the grave.

A healer for the broken.

The hope of the world.

This is our Lord, this is our Christ.

May you know today that God is not through with you—because with Jesus, it is never over, which means *you're* never over. What has ended, my friends, is the long night of death and the power of its sting.

Today is Easter.

Tomorrow is Easter.

Your *entire life* can be Easter.

Wake up. It's morning.

And forever will be.

about the author

There is a movement happening right now in this country. Evangelical Christians, particularly millennials, are looking for two things in the church: authenticity and historicity. They've grown weary of the church "show" and cheap theology. Perhaps because of this desire for authenticity—and my willingness to talk about where I've tried and failed—I seem to connect with those seeking a more ancient expression of the faith in the Episcopal Church, and I am passionate about sharing the Episcopal Church's creative and life-giving liturgy. I am a pastor, writer, and (recovering) lawyer trying hard to express the Christian faith in accessible ways that don't sacrifice the integrity or robust nature of Jesus' love, wisdom, and grace. I believe combining ancient liturgy with modern music and theologically practical sermons is the best way to do this.

I grew up in the evangelical church, attending Pantego Christian Academy during the week and Pantego Bible Church on Sundays. After studying philosophy under the great evangelical and philosopher Dallas Willard at University of Southern California, I returned to Texas for law school and seminary at Southern Methodist University. I practiced law for two years before following my heart to teach and preach. I served as the upper-school religion teacher at All Saints' Episcopal School for three years before joining the staff at Church of the Incarnation in Dallas as the young adults' minister. Two years ago, after a national search for candidates, I was named the lead pastor of the Uptown Services at Incarnation where

I lead three services each Sunday in a one-of-a-kind Gothic chapel designed for modern music that has, on average, more than 700 people in attendance. I have been married to Caroline for six years, and we have two young children, Ford and Charles, both of whom are adorable menaces to society. In my spare time, I am working on a master's in counseling degree because I have a deep conviction the church needs more clergy who are also mental health professionals in order to de-stigmatize and normalize struggles with mental health.

When I'm not working, I can be found wrestling my two savage (and adorable) sons, cheering on the USC Trojans, or eating truckloads of guacamole.

acknowledgments

You don't write a book alone. When I sit down at my desk to write, many people sit with me, people to whom I owe a tremendous amount of gratitude. Without them, I couldn't write a word.

Mom and Dad, I have never known a day without your love and unwavering belief in my dreams.

Caroline, my darling, thank you for "getting" me. Ford and Charles, you won't like this book yet because there are no pictures. But I pray someday you'll read it and know your father loves you just as you are—broken yet perfect.

I want to give a very special thanks to my literary agent, Tina Jacobson, for giving me a shot. I want to thank her even more for becoming such a great friend.

Richelle Thompson, what can I say? You said yes to this book. How can I ever repay you? I can't, but I'll spend the rest of my days trying to write the best words I can to honor your decision. And to the rest of the wildly faithful and talented team at Forward Movement, including Scott Gunn, Rachel Jones, and Jason Merritt, y'all made this happen. Thank you.

Finally, I'd like to thank the Rt. Rev. Anthony J. Burton and the dear people of Church of the Incarnation. Bishop, it's a joy to serve alongside you. Dear people, you have no idea what it means to me that you allow me to enter your lives at your most sacred moments. Your prayers have lifted me up in my time of need. May mine do the same for you.

about forward movement

Forward Movement is committed to inspiring disciples and empowering evangelists. While we produce great resources like this book, Forward Movement is not a publishing company. We are a ministry.

Publishing books, daily reflections, studies for small groups, and online resources are important ways that we live out this ministry. More than a half million people read our daily devotions through *Forward Day by Day*, which is also available in Spanish (*Adelante Día a Día*) and Braille, online, as a podcast, and as an app for your smartphones or tablets. It is mailed to more than fifty countries, and we donate nearly 30,000 copies each quarter to prisons, hospitals, and nursing homes. We actively seek partners across the Church and look for ways to provide resources that inspire and challenge. A ministry of the Episcopal Church for eighty years, Forward Movement is a nonprofit organization funded by sales of resources and gifts from generous donors.

To learn more about Forward Movement and our resources, visit www.ForwardMovement.org or www.VenAdelante.org. We are delighted to be doing this work and invite your prayers and support.